The Rough Guide to

Energy
and our planet

GW00370596

www.roughguides.com

Credits

Written by Context
Design and layout: Peter Buckley, Matthew Milton
Editors: Andrew Lockett, Matthew Milton
Proofreading: Stewart Wild
Production: Rebecca Short

Publishing Information

This first edition published 2008 by
Rough Guides Ltd, 80 Strand, London WC2R 0RL
345 Hudson St, 4th Floor, New York 10014, USA
Email: mail@uk.roughguides.com

Distributed by the Penguin Group:

Penguin Books Ltd, 80 Strand, London WC2R 0RL
Penguin Putnam, Inc., 375 Hudson Street, NY 10014, USA
Penguin Group (Australia), 250 Camberwell Road, Camberwell, Victoria 3124, Australia
Penguin Books Canada Ltd, 10 Alcorn Avenue, Toronto, Ontario, Canada M4V 1E4
Penguin Group (New Zealand), Cnr Rosedale and Airborne Roads, Albany, Auckland, New Zealand

Printed in Italy by LegoPrint S.p.A.
Typeset in Avenir, Minion and Myriad

ISBN 13: 978-1-85828-586-3

ISBN 10: 1-85828-586-0

The Rough Guide to

Energy
and our planet

www.roughguides.com

Contents

Foreword

Never before has humanity faced such a challenging outlook for energy and our planet. This can be summed up in five words: 'more energy, less carbon dioxide'.

Shell is pleased to support this timely Mini Rough Guide, which will promote understanding of our common journey and steps we can all take to enjoy a responsible energy future.

During this century we must reshape the world's energy system to head off dangerous climate change. Renewable energy should make up a larger share of the energy mix, but fossil fuels will still be a major part of it by 2050. We need to find ways of dealing with pollution and greenhouse gas emissions, and new technologies that use less energy to power homes, offices, factories and vehicles.

We can achieve this transformation, but much depends on how soon we start moving to a lower emission energy system. This needs clear thinking, huge investment, and effective leadership.

Energy use is growing faster than ever. Within a few years easily accessible oil and gas will not be able to match this pace of growth. In fact all energy sources together will struggle to meet demand. With more people in the world seeking improved living standards, we'll need energy from lots of sources – renewables such as wind and solar power, biofuels and hydrogen, probably more nuclear power and fuels from 'unconventional' resources such as oil sands that are more carbon intensive to produce. Also, many nations will have few alternatives to using coal to meet their energy needs. As using more energy means more greenhouse gases, we must find ways to manage emissions.

Shell is investing to help deliver the energy the world needs and provide lower-emission energy options, as well as advanced carbon management technologies – but even with huge improvements in energy efficiency and substantial growth in renewables, fossil fuels will still be a major part of the energy mix by mid-century.

Nothing is guaranteed about the future, but in Shell we are using two possible scenarios to help us think ahead. In the first scenario *(Scramble)*, nations secure energy resources for themselves. Policymakers pay little attention to curbing energy use—until supplies run short—and greenhouse gas emissions are not seriously addressed until there are major climate shocks.

In our alternative Scenario *(Blueprints)* growing local actions lead to cross-border cooperation to address the challenges of economic development, energy security and environmental pollution. A price on CO_2 is applied to a critical mass of emissions giving a stimulus to the development of important clean energy technologies and energy efficiency measures. The result is far lower CO_2 emissions. In Shell's view these outcomes are our best hope for a sustainable future.

To learn more about our Energy Scenarios, please visit www.shell.com

Jeremy Bentham
Chief Scenarios Developer, Shell

Introduction

You probably woke up this morning to the sound of the alarm on your clock radio or mobile phone. Then you might have taken a shower, with water heated by natural gas or electricity – which is also probably heating or cooling the rest of your apartment or house. You got dressed, putting on clothes made from cotton gathered by an oil-powered harvester. Your clothes will have been processed and stitched in factories powered by electricity – probably generated from fossil fuels – and then transported, just like the raw materials and the machines that created them, by ship, rail and road, in some cases halfway around the world.

Next, you might go into the kitchen and make a cup of coffee using water pumped from the local water supply (by electricity) and boiled in an electric kettle. The coffee grounds are made from beans grown thousands of miles away, roasted using gas or oil, processed in an electric grinder and shipped to your local shop or supermarket.

Perhaps you travel to an office by train or car. During the day you use computers, printers and photocopiers. On the way home you might pop into a brightly lit shop to buy a ready meal from the chilled cabinet, and heat it in an oven. In the evening you probably watch TV, surf the Internet and listen to music, or go to a cinema, bar or restaurant. Almost every aspect of your life would be unthinkable without convenient modern energy. But there's a very different energy experience that's also still common around the world. Harnessing energy from the environment and getting machines to do our work has largely freed humans in the developed world from the daily toil necessary just to survive. But billions of people still lack such basic energy resources, meaning they spend hours fetching water and gathering wood for fuel and cooking, often in blazing heat.

Ama lives in a small village in Ghana. She wakes up without any alarm clock, just before dawn while it is still cool. She gets up quickly – she has a walk of a quarter of a mile to collect water from the well before the heat gets too strong. She scrubs herself with soap and pours the bucket of water over herself. Her breakfast is made from locally grown maize that she boils in a pan over a wood fire. Ama has no electricity, and transport means walking.

For Ama, life could be a lot easier. If she had electric light she would not have to go to bed at sundown, and could spend time reading, studying or working. There are hundreds of ways in which access to electricity and other forms of modern energy would ease her daily grind. Modern energy would also improve Ama's chances of a long and healthy life: a lack of running water and refrigerated medicines, and exposure to smoke from cooking fires, are some of the biggest reasons why, on average, a person in Ghana lives twenty years less than someone in the developed world.

Over in India, Ranjit's situation is different again. From a poor family, he did well at school and won a scholarship to college. He now works in a large office as a computer programmer. Thanks

Cooking rice in Ghana, West Africa, is a daily grind without the home comforts of gas and electricity.

to his work – in an industry that would not exist without electricity – he is one of millions of Indians for the first time enjoying modern appliances such as televisions, washing machines and air-conditioners, and making regular use of cars. In countries like India, such developments are raising living standards for thousands of people.

Since the populations of today's developed world show no signs of reducing their energy use, the hundreds of millions of anticipated new energy users like Ranjit will significantly increase the total world demand for energy. Meeting this rapidly growing demand for modern energy is one of the major challenges of the twenty-first century – especially as the global population is expected to increase from today's 6.6 billion to more than nine billion by 2050. What makes it harder is the fact that it's becoming increasingly difficult to produce the energy that we have traditionally relied upon. Remaining oil reserves are harder to access, for example, and many of the most suitable positions for hydro-electricity stations, which generate power from rivers, are already in use. Moreover, it's not simply a matter of finding enough energy to go round: there's also the difficult matter of making sure each country has reliable access to secure energy supplies.

Last, but by no means least, we also face pressing environmental problems caused by our energy use, such as local air pollution and, of course, climate change. Human-induced climate change is caused by the release of greenhouse gases, the most important of which is carbon dioxide – which is released whenever oil, coal or natural gas is burned. Energy use accounts for around two-thirds of the total greenhouse gases produced by human activity.

It is a huge challenge to increase energy supplies – and keep them secure – to meet the hopes of people like Ama and Ranjit and to maintain the high living standards of people in the developed world. It is a bigger challenge still to do all this while reducing energy's impact on the environment, including the climate. Both the situation and the solutions are complex. Reading this book will help you understand where we are today and what must be done this century to meet the triple challenge of development, security and environment.

How this book works

This guide will help you get to grips with energy in the twenty-first century. **The Big Picture** explains what energy is, how prosperity depends on it, and explains how a soaring population is rapidly increasing energy demands. It also shows how the energy mix is changing, gives an overview of global energy politics, and addresses the urgent challenge presented by climate change.

Electricity explains how the power grid that brings energy to your home or office works – and how it could work better. It describes how electricity is made today in large, centralized plants using fossil fuels, nuclear power and renewable sources like flowing water and explains how they each contribute to the grid. It also explores the potential of decentralised power-generation and the so-called "energy internet".

Transport shows how important mobility is for social and economic development, and the impacts of today's transport systems on air pollution, congestion and climate change. It looks at some of the new technologies that may get us out of the transport jam.

Staying cool about heating examines the use of energy for heating and cooling, and the new efficiency improvements developing all the time. **Piecing it all together** asks the question on everyone's lips: can we keep the lights on and save the planet? It covers political solutions and explains what you can do. Finally, **Resources** provides details of where you can go to find out more.

01 Energy: the big picture

The basics

What is energy?

Energy is the fuel of life: it makes plants grow; it keeps animals alive; and, in the modern world, it drives devices ranging from medical equipment to space shuttles. A more technical definition would be that energy is the ability of a physical system to do *work*, whether that be growing, lifting, moving or sustaining life.

Humans use many kinds of energy. On a biological level, we get energy by eating plants and animals, and from the warmth of the sun. But over the millennia, we've also discovered more and more ways of exploiting energy (see box opposite). These range from wood fires, which create light and heat from the chemical energy stored in plants, to gas power stations, which create electricity from the heat created by burning natural gas.

A brief history of energy use

Humans have been finding ways to use the energy available in the natural world since prehistoric times. Possibly as long as a million years ago, people worked out how to burn wood, one type of biomass, for heat (for warmth, cooking, and later for smelting metals and making salt) and light (to improve visibility at night and deter dangerous animals).

The next significant developments were related to transport and mechanical work. Around ten thousand years ago, humans learned how to apply the energy of animals to their farmland via ploughs and, as early as 3500 BC, how to use the power of the wind to help move their boats. A few thousand years later, they created mills that could apply the energy of rivers or wind in processes such as grinding grain or pumping water, and also learned how to create light by burning whale oil.

As for fossil fuels, such as oil, coal and gas, it is only in the last two hundred years – since the start of the Industrial Revolution – that they have become the dominant energy source. The rise of fossil fuels was mainly due to their energy density – that is, the amount of energy stored in each litre of fuel. (A litre of coal, for example, contains more than twice the energy as the same volume of wood and a litre of oil much more again.) Another reason was that alternatives such as wood and, by the end of the 19th century, whale oil, were becoming more scarce in areas experiencing rapid industrialisation.

Coal mining took off in Europe in the 17th century, and coal went on to become the main energy source for powering steam engines – the device which helped bring about the Industrial Revolution. Coal also lay behind the birth of the oil industry. In 1846, Abraham Pineo Gesner discovered that coal could be refined to make a flexible, energy-rich transportable liquid fuel called kerosene. Soon after, it was realized that kerosene and other similar fuels – such as gasoline – could be created more easily by refining crude oil, also known as petroleum.

Petroleum quickly became the main transport fuel, but coal remained dominant for heating and the generation of an important new form of energy: electricity. Its use took off in the 1880s after Thomas Edison invented the incandescent light-bulb which was smokeless, easy to use and replaced coal-based gas lamps for lighting in the world's industrialising cities. He built the first power station, which initially lit 59 buildings in New York City.

As the 20th century proceeded, electricity generation became an ever-larger part of the energy picture, thanks to the wide application of electric motors and lights and the fact that it has no smoke or other emissions at the point of use. As time went by, new ways to generate electricity were introduced, including nuclear fission in the 1950s and, more recently, the burning of natural gas and the use of solar and wind farms.

What provides our energy today?

Today, humans exploit many different forms of energy. However, fossil fuels (oil, coal and natural gas) account for around four-fifths of total energy use – a share that has been largely unchanged for the last one hundred years. These fossil fuels dominate because they're relatively cheap, abundant and energy rich, and the global infrastructure is well equipped to produce, deliver and use them.

Different energy sources are used in different sectors. Motorized transport is fuelled almost entirely by oil, while heating is provided by a mixture of gas, oil, wood, coal and other energy sources. As for electricity generation, fossil fuels provide around 67% of the global total, while nuclear and hydroelectricity contribute 15% and 16% respectively. Renewable electricity sources such as solar, geothermal and wind, are growing fast but still constitute only a small percentage (approximately 2%) of the total.

Different countries, different sources

Energy sources and consumption vary hugely from country to country. One factor is what's available locally. For example, China, with little oil and gas of its own, is using its vast coal reserves to help fuel its rapid growth. On the other hand, Japan, which has few natural resources, relies on nuclear power plus imported oil and liquefied natural gas. Canada capitalises on its rivers and mountains to produce hydroelectricity, which is obviously not an option for the low-lying Netherlands.

However, poverty, politics and history are also key factors in the energy used in a country. Around 1.5 billion people cook and heat their homes using traditional "biomass" sources such as wood and animal dung, and travel on foot or using animals. And some countries have large fuel reserves which are mostly exported and consumed overseas.

Workers stack coal bricks at a coal plant in Shanxi Province, China.

What consumes energy?

Whether it comes from fossil fuels, nuclear, hydro or renewables, we use the resulting energy for three broad sectors: industry, transport and buildings. Industrial uses (such as mining, manufacturing, and construction) consume around 37% of the global total. Personal and commercial transportation consumes 20%, while residential and commercial buildings (heating, cooling, lighting, appliances, and the provision of water and sewer services) account for 16%. The other 27% of the energy generated across the world is lost during generation and transmission. We rarely get the most out of the energy sources we use.

According to the International Energy Agency, in 2005 the world used 7,912 Mtoe of energy. That's to say, an amount of energy equivalent to the burning of 7,912 million tonnes of oil – Mtoe being the unit conventionally used to measure large-scale energy use.

More and more of the energy we use is for generating electricity, which will account for almost half of the world's energy

The power of the sun

Ultimately, all energy comes from the sun – mostly through the process of photosynthesis. Without photosynthesis there would be no food (as there'd be no plants and therefore no animals) and no fossil fuels (which are made from the compressed fossilised remains of microscopic plants and animals that lived hundreds of millions of years ago).

Similarly, wind farms are powered by changes in air pressure caused by the uneven distribution of the sun's heat in the atmosphere, and hydro-electric stations are driven by rivers created by the water cycle, which is in turn driven by the sun.

People use the sun's energy directly as well. We trap the sun's rays in green-houses, solar water-heating systems and photovoltaic cells (used to convert the sun's energy into electricity). The ancient Egyptians, like the eco-builders of today, made buildings designed to take full advantage of solar energy.

use over the next 25 years, according to the IEA. Currently the world's electricity is provided for the most part by coal: it accounted for 40% of total electricity in 2005, while natural gas provided 20%, hydro 16%, nuclear 15%, oil just under 7% and renewables 2%. (See p.33 for more on electricity generation.)

Rising demand

Energy demand has almost doubled in the last three decades. It is set to increase by fifty percent by 2030 and could double or even triple by 2050. The demand for gas has increased most rapidly, doubling between 1980 and 2004. There are two factors behind the world's growing thirst for energy – more people and, in particular, more prosperity.

The world's total demand is set to increase at an even steeper rate than the world's rising population. In the last forty years, the world's population has doubled to around 6.5 billion. The rate of population growth is slowing, but it is still high in the Middle East, India, Southeast Asia, Latin America and especially Sub-Saharan

Africa. United Nations forecasters expect the population to top nine billion by 2050, bringing huge energy demands.

Furthermore, as people get wealthier they acquire bigger homes, more appliances and more clothes. Their diets change – incorporating more meat – and they travel more often. This all requires more fuel per person. Globalization also means that raw materials and products travel further.

Meeting demand

So where will all this extra energy come from? At least until 2030, the likeliest answer is still mostly from fossil fuels. We could begin to rely less on fossil fuels as alternative energy sources, such as wind power and hydrogen, become more widely available and economically viable.

Energy and development

Economic growth

Economic growth lifts people out of poverty, giving them access to basic services like electricity, sanitation, clean water and mobility. But these changes require energy, particularly at the early stages as countries go through the transition from pre-dominantly agricultural to industrial economies. As countries industrialize they need to build roads and railways and develop basic industries such as steel which are heavy energy users. The rate of increase eventually slows when more advanced econo-mies reduce reliance on heavy industry and move towards serv-ices and light industry which require less energy, and learn to use energy more efficiently (see p.75).

At present several large countries are going through this early and intensive stage of development – and doing so more quickly than today's economic giants like the US, Japan and Western Europe did a century ago. This is reducing poverty but also means consumption of more materials and more energy. Brazil, Russia, India and China (known as the BRIC countries) are set to become economic leaders by mid-century. China and India are emerging as front-runners, having experienced annual economic growth of around 9.5% and 6% respectively for the past two decades. If their economies continue to soar, India will become the third largest economy (overtaking Germany) and China will bump the US off the top spot by 2040. The IEA predicts that 70% of the increased energy demand to 2030 will come from developing countries. But the other 30% of this growth will be from developed economies, which will also demand more as they get even wealthier, and as their population expands with increasing migration from the developing world.

China and India are now experiencing the most energy intensive period of development, and China alone will account for 30% of that increased energy demand to 2030. (It is still considered a developing nation despite its economic power.) The country's vast size means that no changes there are ever small-scale: the country already has the most mobile phone subscribers (350 million), for example. More Chinese can now afford to own a car – the bicycle, once the ubiquitous mode of transport, is losing out in the cities. In Shanghai in 1980 there were fewer than a thousand private cars: there were over a million in 2006.

Why should we care?

People in emerging economies may be the latest ones to be driving up energy demand – just as people in today's developed world did in previous generations – but this is everyone's concern. The energy market is global, so it doesn't matter where the increased demand comes from. The more demand there is, the higher prices will be for everyone and the more difficult it will be

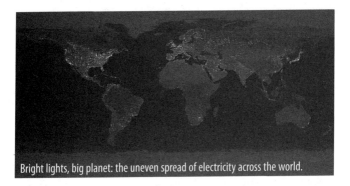

Bright lights, big planet: the uneven spread of electricity across the world.

for countries to guarantee supplies. There is obviously potential for conflict as governments move to secure energy supplies in the face of competition for dwindling resources (see p.22).

Climate change is also a problem for everyone. Energy produced from fossil fuels produces greenhouse gases which are contributing to the planet's rising temperature, bringing floods, higher sea levels and other increasingly serious consequences. It means that national energy use has global consequences. As Kevin Anderson of the Tyndall Centre for Climate Change Research has observed, "the atmosphere doesn't care where the carbon comes from". See p.54 for more on climate change.

Energy disparities

Take a look at a night-time satellite picture of the earth (above) and you'll clearly see the energy haves and the have nots. The developed nations are lit up brightly, while poorer countries show only small clusters of light; much of Africa is a swathe of darkness. This reflects the fact that about 30% of the world's population still live without electricity.

Of the global population, only one in six people have access to the energy necessary for the high living standards enjoyed

13

in developed countries. This billion people use over half the world's energy. By contrast, the billion poorest use only 4%. A comparison of energy use per person highlights just how unequally energy is distributed (see chart below).

China often hits the headlines for its rocketing energy demand, but despite its massive industrial growth, the average Chinese person still uses only a sixth of the average American citizen's consumption. It's also true that China's soaring energy consumption is partly due to manufacturing products for export to developed countries – so it seems a bit rich for those countries to complain about China's energy record.

Following are the figures for 2005 energy consumption per person in various countries, as measured in tonnes of oil equivalent:

USA	7.89	China	1.32
Other OECD countries	4.74	Latin America	1.11
		Africa	0.68
Former USSR	3.44	Asia	0.62
Middle East	2.69	Rest of World	1.78

Energy reserves: how much oil, gas and coal is left?

It took millions of years for the Earth's deposits of fossil fuels to form. We are now using them up faster than we have been finding new reserves. This raises the obvious question of how much is left and when it will run out. But the most relevant question is not when they will run out but when they will become uncompetitive compared to alternatives: when fossil fuels become so difficult and expensive to extract that it becomes cheaper to switch.

Oil and gas will get more expensive to extract as we move

to more remote and more difficult fields, unless technological breakthroughs bring the costs down. On the other hand, wind power and other renewable technologies should continue to get cheaper as they develop. The cheaper the alternatives are, the more quickly people will switch to them.

The higher the price of oil and gas, the more effort companies will invest in ensuring their availability. For example, currently about 60–70% of the oil in most fields remains unexploited in the ground because it has become too expensive to pump out as reserves have depleted. The higher the oil price, the more worthwhile it is for the industry to keep squeezing more out of existing fields.

That's one reason why there is so much disagreement about how much oil and gas there is left. It's not a matter of how much is there, but how much can be extracted economically. According to the International Energy Agency, oil production will peak and start to decline some time in the next thirty years. That's a pretty wide range. But some experts predict it will be sooner rather than later, and others believe we are nowhere near the peak yet (see box overleaf).

Natural gas will probably last longer – there are huge reserves in Qatar, Russia and elsewhere – but supplies are already dwindling in countries such as Canada and the UK. There are vast reserves of coal remaining, but it's the worst pollutant of the fossil fuels. Burning coal can produce severe local pollution as well as the carbon dioxide that contributes to climate change. In the long term coal will only be viable if the technology that cleans up its act can be applied widely enough and cheaply enough (see p.37).

In reserve

When trying to understand fossil fuel reserves, it's important to understand the distinction between the fuel that remains in the ground, and the fuel that can actually be accessed.

Peak Oil theory

The research into the future of oil in our energy mix often discusses the concept of "peak oil". This idea refers to the point at which half of the world's accessible reserves have been extracted. At that point, according to peak oil theory, oil production will start to drop and demand will outstrip supply.

There have been many predictions about when we will reach peak oil. M King Hubbert, the man who devised the theory and illustrated it in a bell-shaped curve, estimated global oil production to peak in 1995. Many industry critics and environmentalists are saying the peak is going to be reached imminently. The International Energy Agency estimated oil production to peak at some point between 2013 and 2037, whereas oil companies tend to argue that, as technology continues to improve and make previously uneconomic deposits profitable to exploit, there will be plenty to go around after that.

For example, you might expect "oil reserves" to mean all the oil that's left in the ground. But experts inside and outside industry use the term to describe only the oil that can be extracted using existing technology profitably in the current market. Reserves are counted commercially only if they are economically recoverable – in other words, companies can make money by pumping the oil out of the ground, refining it and selling it at a price people are willing to pay.

That, in turn, depends fundamentally on the price of crude oil. An oilfield might be profitable with the price at $70 a barrel, but not at $50. And even for a field that is viable at $50, at $70 there is much more that can be done to increase the amount of oil recovered – flushing it with steam or water or CO_2 for example. So as both extraction costs and oil prices vary over time, so will the stated reserves. If we look more broadly at how much oil there is, the US Geological Survey estimates that there is quite a lot more in the ground than we have used so far. But it also estimates that there is plenty more yet to be discovered. However, as the data on the vast bulk of oil supplies are held by OPEC, which keeps a tight lid on its numbers and methods, it is impossible to be sure, as some sceptics have pointed out.

It's not just the volume of oil that's left that we need to worry about. Where it is matters too, and it tends to be concentrated in a few regions, especially the Middle East. The top five countries are: Saudi Arabia, Canada (if you include non-conventional oil), Iran, Iraq and Kuwait.

Non-conventional reserves

Oil doesn't just come in the form of underground lakes and governments are increasingly on the look-out for other sources of oil. There are plenty, and they can be found in politically stable places like the US and Canada. The downside is that it is often difficult, expensive and energy intensive to extract the oil from these other sources.

Oil sands are a mix of clay, sand, water and heavy crude. If found near ground level, it can be dug up and the oil separated from the sands using chemicals and water. It is too expensive to dig up oil sands found deeper underground. Instead the oil can be extracted by pumping steam underground to heat the heavy oil and reduce its viscosity, allowing it to be brought to the surface. Canada and Venezuela have the biggest oil sands reserves.

Oil shale is basically oil that nature hasn't finished making yet. It is a sedimentary rock containing a substance called kerogen that's not buried deep enough or for long enough for time and pressure to produce conventional oil. Give it a few more million years, and it will be oil. If you can't wait that long, you can also provide heat and pressure to speed up the process. It's a complicated and lengthy process and is very expensive. There is plenty of oil shale around - the US government estimates that its oil shales contain one trillion barrels of oil – four times Saudi's proven reserves.

The future contribution of oil sands and shale will depend on various factors, such as oil prices, technological developments, the availability of alternatives and laws relating to carbon emissions. Politics and security of supply will continue to play a part.

The mountains in Rifle, Colorado, are rich in reserves of oil shale.

Remote oil

As fears grow that finding and producing new oil and gas supplies can't keep up with rapidly rising demand, the hunt for new reserves goes wider. New fields tend to be more remote, more complicated geologically, and in pristine areas. This makes them difficult and more expensive to exploit. The Arctic is one example. Up to a quarter of the world's untapped oil and gas reserves are thought to lie under the Arctic. But getting to those reserves has many challenges and they start before drilling even begins. There is the question of how to avoid environmental damage, for example, and the tricky issue of sovereignty: it's not clear which countries own which areas.

A political hot potato

Energy resources have a huge influence over the global economy and politics. It's not hard to see why. Energy is absolutely critical to modern economies, so maintaining consistent supplies is a key priority for most governments. However, the big consumers of energy are not the countries with the big reserves, especially when it comes to oil and gas. Who has the energy and how the others get it is a hot political issue.

The world's oil and gas owners

Oil and natural gas are typically found together, but the proportion varies, so different countries are leaders in each fuel. Saudi Arabia alone possesses a quarter of the world's oil. (Here, we are talking about "proven" reserves, as explained in the previous section.) That is enough to fill more than 130,000 oil tankers. It could supply current world demand on its own for almost a decade. Other countries in the region such as Iran, Iraq and Kuwait are also oil-rich, although not in the same league as Saudi Arabia.

Russia's proven oil reserves are much less, but that's probably only scratching the surface. Eventually it's thought that it could be on a par with some of the Middle East countries. Maybe more importantly, Russia has a huge share of the world's natural gas. Only Iran and Qatar have anything like the same amount. Saudi Arabia, the United Arab Emirates and the US come in further down the natural gas league table.

Looking beyond conventional reserves (see p.15), Canada has more oil than Iran if you were to include the Athabasca oil sands. Venezuela also has large unconventional reserves in the Orinoco oil sands. Add in its conventional crude oil and Venezuela has the largest reserves in the world, as well as the biggest supplies of natural gas in South America.

The US is pretty low down the league of conventional oil but has large reserves of oil shale, although extraction will only be economically viable if the oil price soars (see box on p.17). Algeria and Nigeria are also major oil and natural gas producers. The North Sea now holds relatively little oil, and it's split between the UK, Norway, Denmark, Germany and the Netherlands. Norway's section of the North Sea still has substantial gas fields, however.

Oil and gas dependency

No country in the world (not even Saudi Arabia) is completely self-sufficient in energy. But clearly some countries are more dependent on imports than others. Big economies, such as the US and China, depend heavily on oil imports. After North Sea oil reserves peaked in 1999 the UK also became a net importer again, joining other leading industrial nations. The US uses about 25% of the world's oil, but only has 3% of the remaining proven reserves. China also produces oil, but not nearly enough to meet its total energy needs. Western Europe depends heavily on imported gas, nearly all of it coming from Russia.

The tables opposite show the world's oil, natural gas and coal rankings in terms of both production (not reserves) and consumption. They highlight the fact that the US is still a major oil producer, but that it has nowhere near enough for its needs. The supply/demand picture for coal is different – the big producers such as China, India and the US are also big consumers. Australia is the exception. Despite its own reliance on coal for energy, it is the world's largest exporter, Japan being the main customer.

Energy security

Because energy is so fundamental to modern economies, depending on other countries for it is uncomfortable – especially for the big energy consumers of the developed world, and because oil and natural gas are concentrated in so few countries (see the tables opposite).

Without access to reliable supplies the world's biggest economies would quickly grind to a halt. But no country is energy independent and the need to secure supplies drives governments' energy policies, and can cause international tension.

There are two big priorities for any country: avoiding reliance on politically unstable regions, such as the Middle East, and avoiding reliance on a single source of energy. Diversification is the watchword – different fuel types and different suppliers.

Countries are eager to exploit indigenous resources and to build links with friendly countries. China is a good example. It

Production of natural gas

2006 data (in billion cubic metres)

Russia	656
USA	524
Canada	189
Iran	98
Norway	92

Consumption of natural gas

2005 data (in billion cubic metres)

USA	629
Russia	457
Iran	102
Germany	101
Canada	97

Production of coal

2006 data (in million metric tonnes)

China	2481
USA	1066
India	457
Australia	380
South Africa	244

Consumption of coal

2005 data (in million metric tonnes)

China	2116
USA	1021
India	460
Germany	248
Russia	234

Production of oil

2006 estimates (in thousands of barrels per day)

Saudi Arabia	10,676.75
Africa	10,405.40
Russia	9676.57
Asia & Oceania	8446.76
United States	8370.27

Consumption of oil

2006 estimates (in thousands of barrels per day)

United States	20,587.56
Europe	16,328.65
China	7273.29
Middle East	6157.67
Central & South America	5599.78

is exploiting its own huge coal resources. And it has been forging strong links with African resource-rich countries, controversially including Sudan. India is searching for oil in its own territory, to reduce reliance on imports. Other countries look to alternative fuels. For example, Japan and France have invested heavily in nuclear power as a response to limited domestic resources. Iceland aims to become energy independent by using its domestic hydroelectric and geothermal energy, and by using hydrogen fuel cells to power vehicles. In 2005 the Swedish government announced plans to phase out its use of oil as an energy source via a programme of increased energy efficiency and investing in renewables: it aims to end Sweden's dependence on petroleum, natural gas and other "fossil raw materials" by 2020.

Oil has been one of the big issues in the geopolitics and foreign policies of many nations ever since it became a significant energy source for industrialised countries in the 1930s. The dominance of the Middle East in the world's oil supplies has been a central foreign policy issue for decades, especially for the US since it became a net oil importer in the 1950s. The threat to Kuwaiti supplies after Iraq invaded was an important factor in the first Gulf war in 1990. Similarly, the subsequent invasion of Iraq by the US-led coalition is also often linked to the oil reserves that lie beneath Iraqi soil.

Instability in the Middle East has also affected Europe's energy policies for decades. The threat to oil supplies was a key factor in the Suez crisis in 1956. The first oil shock in 1973 (see p.25) helped persuade the UK and other northern European countries to back development of the North Sea reserves. Having oil in the back yard felt much safer than relying on supplies from countries which could cut supplies for political reasons.

Most battles over energy are "cold wars" – that is, they don't involve any actual fighting. The running battle between the Ukraine and Russia over natural gas supplies is a good example.

In 2005, Russia's state-owned gas company Gazprom cut off supplies to Ukraine in a dispute about prices. Ukraine diverted some of the gas in the pipeline that crosses its land destined for other European countries. This had a knock-on effect on supplies across Europe, and highlighted Western energy dependence on Russia.

The position of Russia as Europe's main natural gas supplier continues to cause ructions. The European Commission is keen to stop Gazprom dominating the continent's gas network. The desire for diversified supplies has led to support for liquefied natural gas terminals in Sicily and Spain to handle fuel from countries such as Nigeria.

Companies and governments

The importance of energy means that governments are big players in influencing both supply and demand. In many cases they are directly involved through state-owned companies. Energy resources belong to the country whose land or sea they lie on or beneath. Most countries originally sold the rights to exploit the reserves to private companies who pay royalties to the government based on the volumes they extract. But governments have always been keen to get the most from their resources, often through companies owned or part-owned by the state. Nationalisation and privatisation have been recurrent themes as countries have looked for a balance between control and maximising revenues. Nationalised companies now produce 85-90% of the world's oil. The biggest national oil company is Saudi Aramco, which took over from international oil companies when Saudi Arabia nationalised oil operations in 1980. Other prominent examples are Russia's Gazprom, CNPC of China, NIOC of Iran, Venezuela's PDVSA, Brazil's Petrobras and Petronas of Malaysia.

By comparison, household-name companies such as

The curse of oil

Governments can amass huge revenues from royalties and other taxes on oil and natural gas extraction. Such huge income can make a big difference to government finances and stimulate economic development, especially in poorer countries. But its value can also stimulate political corruption, with funds being siphoned off or used to benefit a small elite, resulting in greater inequality and conflict. Volatile revenues, such as oil, are hard to manage and can create currency inflation that in turn makes local farms and industry (where most jobs are) uncompetitive. Nigeria is the best-known – but far from the only – example of oil riches increasing tension because oil revenues have not been used adequately to address poverty in the Niger Delta, where the oil and gas are produced.

Corruption can be partly addressed by openness about royalties. If everyone knows how much the government is receiving it is more difficult to explain away the absence of funds for development and other projects. The Extractive Industries Transparency Initiative (EITI) was set up in 2003 by international private, public and voluntary sector organisations to achieve openness on revenues. By April 2006, 26 countries had begun to implement the Initiative and nine had begun reporting revenues – including Nigeria.

ExxonMobil, Shell and BP – the leaders of what is sometimes collectively referred to as "Big Oil" – produce only 10–15% of the world's oil. They are some of the world's biggest private companies, well-known because their names are on the forecourts of service stations all over the world. But they are still dwarfed by the nationalised giants such as Aramco, which are increasingly active beyond their own borders. Aramco is about ten times larger than the biggest of Big Oil, ExxonMobil.

Nationalisation aside, there can still be a tension between governments and private companies, typically when the state believes it is not getting as much revenue from oil or gas production as it should. Venezuela, for example, is estimated to have seized $5.4 billion from international oil companies by renegotiating terms in the past couple of years.

In addition, intergovernmental action can be critical in determining prices and supplies, as shown by the actions of the oil producers' cartel, OPEC (see box).

Climate, environment and energy

In the last decade or so, it has become increasingly clear that human activities – and especially our use of fossil fuels – are causing the planet to heat up. This climate change, also known as global warming, threatens disastrous changes to weather patterns the world over.

We have warmed the climate by boosting a natural phenomenon known as the greenhouse effect, whereby certain gases in the atmosphere trap heat that would otherwise be lost to space. The two most significant greenhouse gases (GHGs) caused

OPEC

The Organization of the Petroleum Exporting Countries (OPEC) is a club of 12 nations: Angola, Algeria, Indonesia, Iran, Iraq, Kuwait, Libya, Nigeria, Qatar, Saudi Arabia, the United Arab Emirates and Venezuela. OPEC has the power to move international markets because it controls 77% of crude oil reserves and 43% of natural gas. In 2006 OPEC countries produced just under half of the world's crude oil.

The organisation acts as a cartel, looking after the interests of its members by agreeing output and oil price targets, and this can have a huge impact on the world economy. In 1973, OPEC cut production of oil and embargoed oil shipments to countries that supported Israel in its conflict with Syria and Egypt. This sparked the first oil crisis and the high inflation of the 1970s when prices increased by 286% in the last few months of 1973. In 1979 there was a second price hike, pushing up the price some 267% from January 1979 to April 1980. The impact contributed to recession in many developed economies.

Bolivian Army soldiers monitor the premises of an oil refinery, following the nationalisation of Bolivia's natural gas and oil industry.

are carbon dioxide (CO_2) and methane (CH_4). Without the greenhouse effect, the planet couldn't sustain life. With it, the temperature averages about 14°C, enabling people, plants and animals to live. Over the past century or so, however, humans have started increasing the levels of GHGs in the atmosphere which are a major cause of climate change.

We may already be experiencing some of the negative effects of climate change. Extreme weather conditions have become more frequent. Droughts have become longer and more intense and heavy rainfall has led to more floods. We've also seen a rise in the intensity of storms. All of these could well be linked to climate change. Unless we act immediately, climate change could have disastrous effects in many parts of the world. The worst case scenario is that at some point "positive feedback loops" could kick in – the world warms enough to release vast amounts

What the IPCC says

The past

- The volume of CO_2 in the atmosphere has increased by 30% since pre-industrial times. That's the fastest change in 650,000 years

- Eleven of the past twelve years were among the hottest since 1850

- Global temperatures increased by 0.74°C in the last century

- Average ocean temperatures have risen so the water has expanded, causing sea levels to rise by 17cm during the 20th century

The future

- It will be between 2.4 and 6.4°C hotter by the end of the 21st century, depending mainly on future greenhouse gas emissions

- Extreme heat will become more frequent and tropical cyclones more intense

- There'll be more rain at high latitudes and less at low latitudes

- Man-made global warming and sea-level rises will continue for centuries even if greenhouse gas emissions were to stop today, but the effects will be more severe depending on future emissions

of greenhouse gases stored in natural "sinks" (such as oceans, forests and soils), causing large temperature increases that in turn dry up other sinks, releasing further trillions of tonnes of CO_2 into the atmosphere.

However, the world would be in trouble well before these types of catastrophes. A 2.4°C increase (see box above) may not sound like much, but it could massively disrupt lives and economies. The best way to reduce this risk is to radically slash our greenhouse gas emissions. Determining what levels of cuts will prevent what likelihood of temperature change is not an exact science. But figures from the IPCC suggest that a global cut of 60% of current levels would give us something in the region of a 70% chance of avoiding 2°C.

chapter 1

A family at home in their village in the North Indian province of Bihar, following floods in Summer 2007.

The scientific consensus

The Intergovernmental Panel on Climate Change (IPCC) is a United Nations body of over 2500 scientists and expert reviewers. It has been assessing scientific information on climate change since 1988. Its Fourth Assessment report, published in 2007, made it clearer than ever that climate change is happening, and it's caused by us.

Where the extra CO_2 is coming from

Fossil fuels such as coal, oil and natural gas are primarily made of carbon – just like the ancient vegetation and creatures from which they come. When the fuel is burned, this carbon combines with oxygen from the atmosphere and is released as CO_2.

The big melt

Changes in the world's ice provide a visible map of climate change. The Earth's largest ice sheets and glaciers are melting as temperatures increase. Satellite images show that Arctic sea ice has shrunk by 2.7% per decade since 1978. And several of the glaciers draining the ice sheets in Greenland and Antarctica have melted dramatically. The poles have seen temperatures increase at twice the global average. As all this ice melts, water is flowing into the oceans, causing sea levels to rise.

Burning fossil fuel is responsible for the majority of carbon dioxide that humans create (the rest comes from deforestation and changes in land use). And the vast majority of that fuel has been burned in the most developed countries since the Industrial Revolution. The "rich world" is responsible for about 70% of the CO_2 in the world today, which explains why there is so much pressure on us to cut emissions even though emerging economies like China and India are expanding fast.

Other environmental issues

Energy use doesn't just release greenhouse gases. Three million people a year die because of emissions from vehicle exhausts and industry (particularly coal-fired power stations). A further 1.6 million are killed by smoke from burning solid fuel indoors for cooking or heating. The victims mostly live in poor countries. Access to modern energy sources in developed nations may have raised the life expectancy of hundreds of thousands of people, but the populations of many developing countries have to rely upon outdated, harmful energy sources in their daily life.

The main pollutants responsible for damaging health are:
• **Sulphur dioxide:** causes tightness of the chest and coughing and severely affects asthmatics. It's released in quantity from

old coal power stations.

- **Nitrogen oxides:** contribute to the creation of ozone, which irritates the lungs and lowers resistance to viruses like flu. They come mainly from road transport and electricity generation, especially from coal.
- **Fine particles:** can be carried deep into the lungs and cause inflammation. Aggravates lung and heart conditions and can be carcinogenic.
- **Carbon monoxide:** colourless, odourless poison gas produced by incomplete fuel combustion, mostly from road transport.
- **Lead:** causes neurological damage in children, affecting memory and attention span. Comes mostly from industrial processes, and from transport in countries where it's not banned in fuel.

Natural gas is the "cleanest" of the fossil fuels, releasing little else but CO_2 and water. Coal is the dirtiest. Traces of toxic heavy elements like mercury and arsenic can be vaporised in coal-fired plants and may become suspended in the atmosphere. In addition, the majority of coal plants release sulphur dioxide, causing acid rain that damages vegetation. Rich countries have more-or-less solved air pollution problems by replacing coal with gas for heating, introducing cleaner vehicles and fuels (see p.57) and cleaning up emissions from coal-fired power plants (see p.37). Poorer countries will be able to invest in these solutions as they develop. Nor are environmental issues confined to fossil fuels. Nuclear power installations have raised substantial environmental concern over waste products whereas large hydroelectric schemes have been criticised for ruining local habitats (see Electricity section). Building energy capacity is rarely without controversy of some kind.

Questions questions

As this chapter has shown, the modern world uses huge amounts of energy and the demand is growing all the time. Energy is literally fuelling the rapid economic development of countries such as Brazil, China and India, just as it drove the industrial revolution in Europe and North America. On a smaller scale, bringing energy to remote villages can transform the lives of people like Ama, whose lifestyle we sketched out in the introduction. But when you look at the big picture, it's clear that there are at least two very important and unanswered questions.

The first question is where we are going to get the energy from to lift people out of poverty while maintaining high qualities of life in developed countries. Any answers to this question must recognise that all countries' energy supplies need to be secure. The world's energy is not distributed evenly – big energy consumers are not big energy producers – so those countries which are energy-rich have a powerful political and economic weapon, and the instability of nations' energy supplies is often a source of international conflict.

The second question is how we're going to deal with the other environmental and social consequences of energy use. At a national level (such as the pollution caused by rapidly expanding coal-fired power stations in China) and at a local level (such as the necessity of cooking using fire inside African dwellings that have no electricity) energy use can have damaging effects. And on a global level, the world must reduce its greenhouse-gas emissions. As we've seen, there is now an overwhelming scientific consensus that the Earth's atmospheric temperature is increasing dangerously, and that something must be done. Moreover, many governments are nervous about imposing significant reductions targets – because they don't want to restrict economic growth or impose disadvantages on their industry in a global economy. In short, by 2050 we need twice as much energy as we do today, but with no increase in CO_2 levels.

And so we reach the million-dollar question: how to avoid countries running out of energy but at the same time avoid disastrous environmental damage? The answers involve a combination of technology, economics, politics, education and social change. That is how most developed countries have successfully dealt with local pollution, whether from domestic fires, cars or power stations. It can also be dealt with elsewhere, but poverty will often stand in the way.

Meeting the climate change problem is much more difficult. Some people believe the answer is a drastic change in lifestyles and a development model to slash energy demand. Then there those who think we can simply invent our way out of the dilemma with new technology. The solution is probably somewhere in between these extremes. It has been described clearly in the Stern Report, commissioned by the UK Government, which suggested we could cut carbon dioxide emissions from energy through a combination of taxes, innovation and technology, in addition to halting deforestation. Sir Nicholas Stern acknowledged the difficulties and the costs. But he also stressed that while there will be losers, especially in industries that rely on carbon-intensive fuel, there will also be new opportunities – in businesses ranging from wind turbines to insulation.

The following chapters take a look at how these unanswered questions relate to specific areas: electricity, transport and heating and cooling.

02 Electricity

Electricity is an integral part of life in developed countries, powering everything from the appliances in our homes to the computers in our offices – not to mention countless industrial processes. Of course, electricity isn't an energy source – it has to be generated from other sources such as fossil fuels, nuclear reactions or the movement of water or the wind. Rather, it's an extremely useful energy carrier.

The grid and how it works

Most of us only give thought to the distribution of electricity on the rare occasions when we flick a switch and nothing happens – in a power cut, for instance. However, the electricity that we take for granted relies on an immense network of power stations and transmission lines connected into a "grid" and operated with immense care.

The way the grid is set up means that consumers are not dependent on any one specific power station (or hydroelectric dam or wind turbine). The electricity from different sources is pooled together via a network of cables to provide a reliable supply. So if one power station or transmission line is taken out of service, consumers will usually not be affected. It also means that fluctuating demand can be met – the different requirements of different end users change every second and the grid has to be able to cope.

One problem with distributing electricity via cables is that some of the power – around 7% of the total – is wasted through transmission losses. To keep this to a minimum, the high-capacity cables that carry the bulk of the power (the ones you see slung between pylons) operate at very high voltages. The voltage is reduced to safer and more useful levels in local substations before the electricity is distributed to end users.

Supply and demand

There is still no practical way to store electricity on a large scale. For this reason, electricity is generated to meet demand as and when. But demand fluctuates widely – for example, there's always a surge during half-time of a televised soccer cup final when everybody switches on the kettle. As such, the transmission system is constantly adjusted at computerised control centres to match supply with demand.

The grid divides power stations into three categories: **base load**, **intermediate load** and **peak load**. Base load stations are in constant use and provide the minimum amount of power needed. Nuclear plants, coal-fired power plants and hydro often take this role. They are slow to start up and shut down and expensive to build, but they are cheap to run. In the case of hydro, the running costs are virtually zero.

Intermediate load stations are brought on line when power demand is higher. Peak load stations tend to be gas-fired: they are quick to start up and cheap to build, but more expensive to run.

Electricity from fossil fuels

About two thirds of the world's electricity is produced by burning fossil fuels. Nuclear and hydropower provide almost all of the rest. The amount of electricity derived from alternatives such as wind, solar power and geothermal energy is increasing quickly, but they currently form a very low base – approximately two percent of today's electricity. Fossil fuels are likely to be around for a long while yet – they are the cheapest and most convenient power source. So one major energy challenge is to make

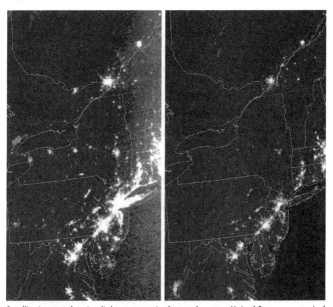

Satellite images showing light coverage in the northeastern United States on a typical night (left); and after a massive blackout affected much of the area (right), shown at 9:03 PM Eastern time on August 14, 2003 due to the power outage.

these power plants as efficient and environmentally friendly as possible.

Coal alone produces about 40% of the world's electricity (see below). Use of natural gas has been growing fast since the 1980s thanks to high efficiency turbine technology and its lower pollution levels, while oil is increasingly being phased out of electricity generation. Today's electricity-generating technologies are long-established and reliable but new technologies are available which are more efficient and cleaner. One obstacle to their implementation is that power stations typically have working lives of fifty years or more – so change on the ground is relatively slow.

Burning coal for electricity

Coal was the first fossil fuel to power stations in most countries and it still does in many – particularly those with large reserves. The main advantages of coal are that it's cheap and in plentiful supply – especially in countries such as the US, Australia, India and China. The disadvantage is that it's the dirtiest and least climate-friendly of the fossil fuels. A modern coal power plant emits around twice as much CO_2 as a modern gas-fired. That is both because they are less efficient (see above) and because the coal itself contains more carbon per unit of energy. Coal power stations also emit other pollutants: nitrogen oxide (NOx) contributes to acidification of lakes and streams (acid rain); sulphur oxide (SOx) can substantially aggravate asthma and chronic bronchitis; and mercury can cause severe nervous system problems in humans and wildlife, to which developing foetuses, babies and children are especially vulnerable. For example, a study of individuals exposed to smoky coal emissions from cooking and heating their homes in Xuan Wei County, China, found that they could well have experienced damaging genetic mutations that greatly increase their risk of developing lung cancer.

Power plant efficiency

The efficiency of a fossil fuel-fired power plant lies in how much of the energy stored in its fuel is converted to electricity. Efficiency has been gradually improved over the years.

Many traditional coal-fired power plants are only about 30% efficient, meaning that more than two-thirds of the energy content of the input fuel is lost as waste heat, instead of being turned Into usable electricity. By comparison, modern natural gas-fired Combined Cycle Gas Turbines have an efficiency approaching 60%. These work by capturing much of the waste heat and using it to generate additional electricity. Instead of first making steam, the turbines get turned directly from the hot flue gases from burning the natural gas. Combined heat and power (CHP) plants achieve even better efficiencies – between 65% and 80% – than conventional generation because they use the waste heat either to drive industrial processes or to heat buildings. They can use any fuel source, as CHP can be used with a conventional steam turbine.

Various "clean coal" technologies help improve coal's environmental performance. For example, pulverising coal means that it can be burned more completely at higher temperatures, creating more electricity and less waste. Chemically treating fuel to eliminate minerals and impurities helps reduce emissions of pollutants such as NOx, SOx and particulates. These technologies are used in many countries to meet local air pollution targets and they can be retrofitted for use in existing power stations although this is expensive. Coal gasification also makes coal cleaner. Coal is converted to a synthesised gas, which is a more efficient and cleaner source of heat. A more ambitious "clean coal" aim is to capture the CO_2 and store it underground (see box overleaf).

Natural gas

In many countries since the 1970s, coal-fired electricity production has grown more slowly than from other sources. For example, the UK experienced a "dash for gas" in the late 1980s. In gen-

Sequestrating the CO_2 from fossil fuels

However cleanly and efficiently you can burn fossil fuels, they'll always produce CO_2. But the technology exists to separate and capture that CO_2 and stop it entering the atmosphere – a process known as sequestration or carbon capture and storage.

The aim is to capture the CO_2 as it is generated and store it underground in depleted oil and gas wells or saline aquifers – or use it in other industrial processes. At the pressures and temperatures found right hundred meters or more underground, CO_2 liquefies enough to stay where it is, rather than coming

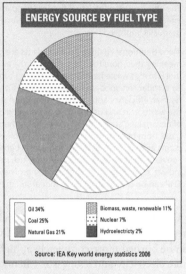

ENERGY SOURCE BY FUEL TYPE

▫ Oil 34%	▨ Biomass, waste, renewable 11%
▨ Coal 25%	⋯ Nuclear 7%
▪ Natural Gas 21%	▪ Hydroelectricty 2%

Source: IEA Key world energy statistics 2006

back up to the surface. Several carbon capture and storage experiments are underway, but so far that's all they are – experiments. It may be a while before sequestration is feasible on a wide scale and new coal power stations with built-in sequestration probably won't emerge before 2020.

Even when it works, carbon capture and storage isn't cheap. For a typical coal-fired power plant, it would mean extra investment of hundreds of millions of dollars. The US Department of Energy estimates that sequestration would cost something in the region of $50 per tonne of CO_2 emissions avoided using current technology. It is investing heavily in research and development, with the aim of reducing this price to $10 per tonne by 2015.

erating power, natural gas produces about 30% less CO_2 than oil and about 50% less than coal. However, in many Western countries gas resources are diminishing. Western Europe produces only 60% of what it needs, mostly from the British, Dutch and Norwegian reserves in the North Sea. Much of the remainder is imported from Russia, through the Ukraine (see p.22–23).

Nuclear power

In one memorable episode of *The Simpsons*, Lisa and Bart go fishing near the Springfield nuclear plant and catch a three-eyed fish they name Blinky. Radioactive waste from the nuclear plant had created a whole new mutant sub-species. The episode reflects widespread anxieties about nuclear power, which remains controversial over half a century after it was first used to generate electricity. Accidents at Three Mile Island in the US and Chernobyl in the Ukraine stimulated safety fears and there are other concerns, too.

Waste is one, because it remains radioactive (and therefore dangerous) for thousands of years – and there is no permanent solution for storing it that is guaranteed to stay safe. Cost is another. Generating nuclear power is pretty cheap once you've built the power stations. But the cost of construction, and the time involved, are very significant. Then there is the cost of dealing with the waste. And the worry about nuclear fuel falling into the hands of terrorists. Things are further complicated by political tensions – the stand-off between Iran and the US in 2007 is a good example. Iran argues it is entitled to develop nuclear power; the US says this is a prelude to making nuclear weapons, and must be stopped.

Currently, 16% of the world's electricity is nuclear. It is dominant in countries such as France (where 59 reactors generate 78% of the country's electricity) and the US, which is the world's biggest nuclear producer (104 reactors producing a fifth of its electricity). Japan also uses a lot of nuclear power, helping the country reduce its dependence on imported fuels.

Transporting gas by sea

One major difficulty with natural gas is that it is expensive to move it around – unlike coal or oil which can be transported by ship. It is typically moved through pipelines, which are cost-effective on land – even over relatively long distances such as Russia to Western Europe – but impractical under the ocean.

This is a problem because (as with oil) natural gas sources are not widely distributed around the world. Fifteen countries produce 84% of the world's gas. There is a large international market and hence a need to transport the gas over the oceans.

The answer is to turn the gas to a liquid by cooling it down to minus 162 celsius. That means it takes up six hundred times less space – making it economical for the liquefied natural gas (LNG) to be transported across oceans in tankers, then turned back into gas at the other end. Many countries in Europe have recently joined Japan in contracting LNG imports from Qatar.

LNG makes gas supply more secure for countries that are currently dependent on pipelines or, like Japan, beyond a pipeline's reach. But it is expensive to build the processing plants and other infrastructure required, which has meant that suppliers have looked for contracts as long as thirty years to provide the confidence needed to justify the investment.

Nuclear's case has been strengthened by environmental concerns. It does not produce the local pollution that is a problem with coal. It produces far fewer carbon emissions than fossil fuels, to the extent that it is promoted as carbon-free and has recently been supported by some environmentalists on this basis. The British scientist James Lovelock, father of "Gaia theory" is a former opponent of nuclear power, but now argues that it is key to fighting global warming, and says fears about nuclear power have been over-hyped.

Others dispute nuclear power's "carbon-free" tag. It's true that nuclear plants emit only negligible amounts of CO_2 in use, but the mining, processing and transportation of uranium and the storage of its waste all release greenhouse gases. There are also

Workers suiting up to begin a shift to decontaminate Three Mile Island's Unit 2 reactor in Middleton, Pennsylvania in 1988 (nine years after an accident at the plant).

many who point out that the cost of building nuclear power stations is money that is better spent on renewable energy technology: Amory Lovins suggested that nuclear expansion is "buying less solution per buck". But there are also many who say that nuclear waste is a poor environmental legacy to hand to our children – and hence is not an acceptable solution.

Renewable electricity

There are plenty of sources of electricity that aren't nuclear and aren't fossil fuels. They lie in the four elements which humans have used ever since they began sailing boats and drying skins: water, air, fire and earth.

Hydroelectric power is a well-established use of water (see box on p.43). Other sources of energy from water may become more important in future. For example, **wave energy** can be extracted and converted into electricity by wave power machines. The main problem is that the sea is not an easy environment in which to operate machinery. An economically viable wave power machine will need to generate power over a wide range of wave sizes, as well as being able to withstand the largest and most severe storms and other potential problems such as algae, barnacles and corrosion. **Tidal energy** exploits the natural ebb and flow of coastal waters. The coastal water level fluctuates twice daily, alternately filling and emptying natural basins along the shoreline. The currents flowing in and out of these basins can be exploited to turn mechanical devices to produce electricity. In order to produce practical amounts of electricity, a difference between high and low tides of at least five metres is required.

Wind is another source of energy that can be converted to electricity using turbines driven by propeller-like blades. The turbines are typically positioned on high ground to benefit from stronger, more consistent wind speeds, or at sea ("offshore"), where winds tend to be even stronger, more consistent and the turbines can be larger (and out of sight).

Then there's the sun, which is the indirect source of all our energy (see p.10). It is a vast source, producing thousands of times more energy every day than we use. This **solar** energy can be turned into electricity using **photovoltaic (PV) cells** or using technologies which direct the sun's heat into water, creating steam to turn turbines. Finally, the Earth provides renewable energy in the form of crops, wood and other organic materials that can be burned to create steam for electricity or used to produce energy-rich gas through decomposition. Known collectively as **biomass**, this can also include waste from animals, food or industrial processes, as well as fast-growing algae. In addition, the Earth offers **geothermal** energy in the form of heat stored underground. This can be used to power electricity generators

– it's currently more widely associated with heating buildings but it's a source that has plenty of potential (see p.80).

Hydroelectricity

Hydroelectricity now produces 16% of the world's electricity (a bit more than we get from nuclear power). Hydroelectric dams use the energy from water in fast-flowing rivers, or from man-made installations, where water from high-level reservoirs flows down and turns a turbine. There is a limit to how much it can be expanded as many rivers that are naturally suited to hydroelectric generation have been exploited already. Hydroelectric projects can be problematic as they can damage aquatic ecosystems and disrupt river flows, affecting water supplies for people living downstream. And local populations often have to be relocated to build new reservoirs for man-made hydroelectric stations. But, beyond the initial carbon footprint of building the dam, hydroelectricity generation produces no CO_2 emissions, so it's a climate-friendly alternative to fossil fuels.

The Niagara River Gorge is situated on the United States-Canadian Border: on the left is the Ontario Hydro power plant and on the right is the Robert Moses power plant.

Pluses and minuses

The attraction of these renewable energy sources is that they meet all three of the key requirements set out at the beginning of this book: meeting growing energy demand; increasing energy security; and avoiding further environmental damage, such as carbon dioxide emissions.

That is why huge amounts of political effort as well as finance and research are being poured into growing the contribution of renewables. Today non-hydro renewables supply about 2% of the world's electricity. The sector is growing fast but even so it is likely to provide only about 15% by 2030.

There are problems to be overcome. For many renewables, the most basic problem is the unreliability of the weather. What happens when the sun doesn't shine, the wind doesn't blow, or the sea is too calm? Power stations can control when and how much power they produce but we can't control the elements, even if we can harness them.

Even when these challenges are overcome, there are other complicating factors as well. First, there's cost. The wind, sun and sea might be free, but turning their power into electricity certainly isn't. Generating solar or wave power can cost as much as twenty cents per kWh, compared to as little as three cents for power from a conventional coal-fired power plant. Wind power is much closer to being competitive but still struggles to get as low as coal or gas: it can cost as little as six cents at the best onshore sites but costs twice that offshore. Costs should come down further as technology develops, but it may take a while. So, for now, wind energy is growing mainly on the back of government subsidies.

There's also the question of scale: can we put up enough solar panels and wind turbines fast enough to generate a substantial share of the energy we need? A turbine typically generates no more than 3MW (although they can be more powerful offshore), which produces enough electricity for less than two thousand typical European homes. Hundreds of thousands will be needed if wind energy is to grab a substantial share of the electricity cake. And that brings us to another problem: many people don't want them built near their homes, a phenomenon known as NIMBYism – "Not In My Back Yard". This is a powerful factor in delaying the spread of wind turbines, although one that should be less and less significant as cabling technology enables them to be placed in increasingly remote places.

Thinking small

Ama doesn't have electricity sockets in her house. One solution to her problem is to extend the grid to villages like hers, but that is expensive and could take decades. An alternative might be the use of a local power source, such as small-scale solar or wind. There's plenty of sun in remote African villages, and if it can be captured during the day and stored in simple batteries, it can be used at night. This is cheaper than extending the grid and in some cases cheaper than buying kerosene for lighting. But it still requires a bigger one-time investment than people like Ama can afford even if it's shared with neighbours – a domestic solar system could light three to six rooms and power a black-and-white TV each night, but it would cost more than $500. Rolling out these type of off-grid solutions in the developing world will require massive amounts of investment.

The success of the Internet in reinventing telecommunications has led to the idea of reinventing the electricity grid along the same lines. Just as Internet pundits talk of "user-generated content", the grid would be based on user-generated power. This idea – that of the smart grid – is predicated upon smart meters that provide users with extremely detailed information about the power their appliances are using and can track the power they are producing and sending back to the grid. Some are predicting smart grid networks that could link millions of distributed energy devices such as solar panels, wind turbines, smart appliances and even electric vehicles, whereby household-generated energy could be fed back into the grid.

Forget dependence on remote generation. Forget terrorist threats to power stations. Why shouldn't each household be a mini-power station, generating its own electricity? When you need more you can buy it from the grid; when you've got more than you need you can export it to the grid and get paid for it by a power company. Npower and Good Energy are two companies that currently pay for micro-generated power. There are a variety of ways to generate electricity on a local level. All of them help minimise transmission losses, since the electricity is generated at the point of consumption, and most of them help reduce carbon emissions too, as fewer transmission losses means less CO_2 per KWh.

Combined heat and power

A combined heat and power (CHP) plant doesn't have to be huge. Micro-CHP is like a super-efficient miniature power station. Fuel is burned to create electricity, and the by-product – heat from combustion – is captured and used for space and water heating. Any excess electricity generated can be fed back into the grid.

Gas is the most common fuel for small-scale CHP, due to its convenience and relatively low price and emissions. But other fuels such as wood are also used. Micro CHP units are already used in some commercial buildings but, so far, they're rare in households because of high capital cost, space requirements and local fire regulations.

Fuel cells

Fuel cells have been most closely associated with cars, using hydrogen, but they may have greater potential for stationary power generation – in the short-term, at least. A cell produces energy through chemical reactions, like a conventional battery, but from a stream of fuel. So emissions are negligible but the cell provides a constant power source. Many fuels can be used, including natural gas and gasified biomass as well as hydrogen.

Micro renewable generation

Renewable domestic power generation is possible but currently uneconomical in most cases: the cost of buying and installing equipment such as solar panels or wind turbines is unlikely to be recouped for many years.

Solar thermal heating is becoming more widely used for hot water (see p.10), but the cost of photovoltaic material needs to fall further to make electricity-generating solar panels financially attractive for most homes, especially in climates where there may be limited hours of sunlight. As for micro wind turbines, they can be effective in rural areas but are unlikely to generate sufficient power in cities where wind speeds and patterns make them less effective.

Another issue is that electricity grids were designed to feed power from centralised generators to users. Widespread micro-generation with two-way transmission is technically possible but will require a new attitude to running the grid, and new financial arrangements. Utility companies would no longer be paid primarily for the amount of electricity they supply, but for managing the grid.

In countries where awareness of climate change is high, some politicians have started advocating micro-generation, and offering public funds to subsidise solar and other technologies. In

Germany users are paid a premium for feeding power back into the grid. Elsewhere, however, there's often little political will to create a decentralised grid and minimal financial incentive for householders to invest in micro-generation. In some countries, householders who sell energy into the grid receive only about a third of the price they are charged when they buy power. Other countries have looked to encourage consumers to use less electricity – ideas for which are discussed on p.83.

03 Transport

Planes, trains and automobiles … it would be hard for most of us to imagine modern life without motorised transport. Even if we stay at home, we need food, clothes and other goods; and these things don't just walk in the door themselves – many reach us from the other side of the world via ships and delivery trucks. Around 30% of global energy use can be attributed to transport, of which nearly all is currently provided by petroleum-based products such as petrol, kerosene and diesel. This translates as some 60% of the world's crude oil production being used to fuel the world's transport.

Partly due to economic and population growth in developing countries, demand for transport fuels is rising all the time. Each day more people are joining this world of modern transport – replacing, for example, a two-hour walk to work with a 20 minute bus or scooter ride – so that they can get to the urban centres where the better-paid work is. The fuels that propel these journeys won't last indefinitely, however, and they already contribute significantly to local air pollution in developing countries

– with old engine technologies and dirty fuels – and to climate change everywhere. What's more, it is expected that by 2050, 80% of the world's population will have gravitated to urban areas from the current level of 50%. This will generate even more demand for transport, more GHGs and, unless advanced engine and fuel technologies spread to the developing world, more local air pollution. So the world is faced with the dual challenge of meeting the growing demand for transport, while also developing more environmentally friendly vehicles and fuels.

Transport and development

Economies and population

As with most aspects of energy use, there are two big trends behind the growth in transport: rising populations and economic development. The latter affects transport in various ways. First, as an economy switches from agricultural to industrial, people and goods move about more. Locally, people travel to factories instead of working in the fields or at home. Globally, materials and products travel further. At the same time, as people get more money and leisure time, they want to travel more and to travel more conveniently, and there's a tendency to make more discretionary trips – especially flights and holidays. The really significant step, however, is being able to afford private cars, the use of which typically replaces journeys made by public transport, bicycle or by walking.

Car ownership and use

The figures speak for themselves. In 1950 there were about eighty million vehicles on the world's roads. Fifty years later, at the start of the twenty-first century, that figure had risen to nine hundred million. Add another fifty years, to 2050, and it's estimated there will be over two billion cars on the roads. And while new cars in the developed world have become dramatically cleaner – their fuel efficiency hasn't. The average fuel efficiency of today's cars is about the same as that of the Model T built by Henry Ford back in 1908.

Car ownership is rising fastest in the developing world. The BRIC countries (Brazil, Russia, China and India) are expected to account for almost half of passenger car sales during this decade. In China, there were 24 cars to every thousand citizens in 2006. By 2010, that will have risen to forty. That's still lower than in the developed world – according to the UN Economic Commission for Europe, in 2002 the US had 765 vehicles for every thousand citizens – but with China's population of 1.3 billion, it still translates to 21 million extra cars, requiring approximately thirteen million barrels of oil every time they fill up their tanks. It's a similar story in the Indonesian capital city Jakarta.

The car is beginning to oust the bicycle as China's favourite mode of transport.

In 1990, there were 1.6 million vehicles on the streets. Ten years later that had climbed to 4.2 million. If car ownership in China, India and Indonesia were to equal the world average of ninety cars per thousand people, 200 million vehicles would be added to the global fleet.

So why are private cars so appealing, even when they're not the quickest transport option and we all suffer from the problems they generate? The answer encompasses status, safety, comfort, independence, and the convenience of point-to-point autonomous travel.

Public transport

In addition to concerns over energy security, local air pollution and climate change, rising car use is raising the problem of congestion. Traffic jams curse virtually every city in the world from time to time, but in places like Jakarta, the authorities have had to resort to a "three-in-one" car policy to encourage car sharing during rush hour. Elsewhere, other government initiatives have been introduced, such as London's Congestion Charge, which taxes cars that drive into the city centre. There have even been schemes introduced in some cities where only odd or even numbered licence plates can be driven on certain days – though this often encourages people to buy a second car!

The obvious answer is a switch to public transport. A hundred people on a bus, or several hundred on a train, take up far less space and use less energy than the same number of people in private cars. However, public transport systems require new infrastructure that takes time to approve and build and, unless they are managed well on a day-to-day basis, they can create more problems than they solve. The real issue, however, is the world's love affair with the private car, and the knock-on result that politicians seeking to prioritise bus and tram networks over private cars often meet with fierce resistance from voters.

Freight transport

Cars are not the only drain on the world's fuel. Just think how they get to the showrooms – on ships across the oceans and transporters across the land. In both the developing world and in developed countries trucks provide the backbone of freight transport. In developing countries, often old, overloaded or poorly serviced, trucks guzzle diesel and frequently belch filthy exhaust gases. Many of these trucks are hand-me-downs from affluent countries – an unfortunate example of where improvements in the developed world displace problems to developing economies, which can't afford the lower polluting and more fuel-efficient modern vehicles.

Air travel

The rapid growth of flying is another concern – especially when considering climate change. Globalization has driven growth in business flights, while the increase in air travel for leisure and holidays abroad is a consequence of greater affluence and more affordable fares. Take the UK in 2006, when some 235 million passengers passed through Britain's airports. By 2030, the UK government predicts that figure will have gone up to 500 million.

One factor in such growth is the emergence of budget airlines, which have carved out a significant share of the market. The capacity of low-cost airlines more than doubled between 2002 and 2006, rising from 22 million seats on 169,000 flights to 46 million seats on 323,000 flights. As airline tickets have become cheaper and cheaper, demand has increased.

Transport, climate change and the environment

The vast majority of cars, trucks, ships and planes – and still many trains, too – are powered by oil. As we'll see later on in this chapter, alternatives such as bioethanol and hydrogen fuel cells are only just beginning to emerge, which both reduce the environmental impact of transport and strengthen the security of supply. But for now, as for the last century, the internal combustion engine rules supreme on the roads, and there's no sign of a promising alternative to the jet engine for planes. All these oil-powered engines have a major impact on the environment – both on a global level, through climate change, and at a local level, through air pollution. Alternatives have a tough job to compete with oil-derived fuels, which are widely available, cheaper, energy-dense, easy to transport in bulk, store and transfer to vehicles. In short, there are not yet any scaleable or affordable alternatives and the cost effectiveness, existing global infrastructure (pipelines, storage depots, retail stations) and wide availability of the internal combustion engine perpetuate the use of oil-based fuels.

Climate change

Vehicles make a large contribution to the greenhouse emissions that cause climate change. Almost a quarter of human-created CO_2 emissions (roughly 14% of total greenhouse emissions) are accounted for by transport. Though transport isn't the largest GHG source (electrical power generation accounting for almost double the amount) it is the fastest growing and the most difficult and expensive to reduce. In the US, the Energy Information Administration estimated that transport accounted for 33% of all energy-related carbon dioxide emissions. Almost all of those transport emissions – 98% – came from the use of petroleum products such as petrol, diesel and jet fuel. In the coming decades the level of greenhouse gas emissions from transport is expected to rise steeply, as global car use increases.

Road transport accounts for around three-quarters of all transport emissions. In 1950, seventy million tonnes of CO_2 emissions were produced on the world's roads. In 2000, the emissions had risen to over a gigatonne – a whopping one billion tonnes. Add another fifty years and it gets a lot worse. By 2050, the estimated two billion road vehicles could produce up to three gigatonnes of CO_2 based on the current average fuel efficiency of vehicles.

The exact impact of aviation on the climate is hard to pin down, since it depends not just on CO_2 emissions but also on the impact – at high altitudes – of other gases such as nitrous oxide. Even water vapour emissions from jet engines could be significant, since they cause cloud trails ("condensation trails" or "contrails") behind planes, which themselves may have a warming effect, especially when released at night.

There is still no definitive figure, but scientists believe the overall climate impact of aviation is at least double that of the carbon dioxide emissions alone. The IPCC estimates that air traffic could currently be responsible for around 5% of the total human contribution to climate change. It is the developed nations that are responsible for the majority of it.

New planes are significantly more efficient and load factors are rising, so emissions per passenger can be expected to decrease. But aviation is worrying because it's growing so fast. According to some estimates, if this growth isn't slowed, air travel alone could account for all of the UK government's target level of greenhouse gas emissions by 2050.

Local air pollution

In the developed world, advances in fuel and engine technology, together with government regulations, have reduced transport's contribution to local air pollution levels dramatically. Total emissions from vehicles in the EU, for example, have dropped by over 70% in a decade – even though transport kilometres continue to rise.

Until fifteen years ago, you would probably have filled up your car with leaded petrol. Lead had been added to almost all petrol for decades to help engines run better, but it was eventually shown to damage people's health. For example, lead can cause anaemia, which reduces the body's ability to circulate oxygen and vital nutrients. Refiners found replacements for lead, and engine designs have now been adapted to run well without leaded petrol. This development paved the way for the reductions of other exhaust chemicals, too. For example, it allowed petrol vehicles to be fitted with catalytic converters, which convert carbon monoxide, hydrocarbons and nitrogen oxides into CO_2, nitrogen and water. Similarly, it allowed diesel vehicles to be fitted with particulate traps, which filter out and oxidize tiny particles linked to lung cancer and asthma.

Petrol and diesel also contain sulphur. When we burn these fuels in our cars, the sulphur forms sulphur oxides that contribute to local smog and to acid rain, which damages vegetation and pollutes rivers and streams. Sulphur is now nearly completely removed in the oil refining process, which avoids environmental damage and makes catalytic converters and particulate traps work more efficiently. However, this process takes a lot of energy at the point of manufacture, which means more CO_2 emissions. On the plus side, it's easier to capture these emissions from a single more concentrated source at the refinery than from car exhaust systems.

But the story is still very different in many less developed countries where vehicle fleets are older, and the money is not available to upgrade refineries to make unleaded and low sulphur fuels. Technology and development are clearly the answer here. Over time, as these countries grow more prosperous, they will be able to afford the cleaner gasoline and diesel, and the engine technologies that have so dramatically improved air quality in today's developed world.

Solutions: the road to greener transport

So, can the world solve the transport conundrum, keeping people and goods moving while simultaneously improving air quality in the developing world and cutting CO_2 emissions? That remains to be seen, but with the right mixture of technology, politics and behavioural change, the goal is certainly not impossible. There is plenty that we can all do by making greener choices about how we travel, and we look into these in the Piecing It All Together chapter (see p.74). But there have already been some significant technological developments in transport that are rising to the challenge.

More efficient vehicles

One key strategy in reducing the energy required by transport is to get more miles out of each litre of fuel. We already know how to make efficient vehicles. Some family cars do close to fifty miles per gallon, but most are far less economical. The main reason for this is that, at least until the recent rises in fuel prices, customers have been voting with their wallets for bigger and more powerful cars. For example, American freeways are full of SUVs (sports utility vehicles), big, heavy and with poor aerodynamics, which have also been growing in popularity in other countries. These heavy, four-wheel-drive cars are sometimes only capable of as little as 13mpg. One useful response to the problem would be for individuals to switch to diesel-engine vehicles. While the challenge of diesel was once its high local emissions, this problem has now been solved. Switching from gasoline to diesel would result in 25–30% fuel efficiency improvement – and improve engine performance.

Hybrids and electric cars offer another route to greater efficiency. In 1997, Toyota broke ranks with its peers when it launched the first mass-production "hybrid" car – the Prius. Hybrid cars have an electric motor, which supports the regular petrol engine. The motor is powered by an onboard battery pack that is charged partly by energy from braking that would otherwise be wasted and by the petrol engine when it is used. The hybrid system means that the Prius tops its class in fuel efficiency, without compromising on power. Various hybrids have followed in the footsteps of the Prius, including the Honda Insight, which, being smaller and lighter, achieves even lower fuel consumption and emissions.

Cars completely powered by electricity also exist. They're plugged in and charged up via the mains, just like mobile phones and other rechargeable devices. Even when you factor in the emissions involved in generating the electricity, electric cars result in less total CO_2 per mile than the alternatives, due to the conversion efficiency of the electric engine. What's more, they don't even have exhaust pipes, so produce no local pollution. On the flipside, current electric cars are either expensive – such as the $80,000 Tesla sports car – or limited in speed and range.

Individuals can already opt to buy greener – cleaner or more fuel efficient – petrol-fuelled cars, of course. But large-scale improvements in vehicle efficiency are mainly driven by minimum standards set by governments in consultation with the motor industry. In China, the authorities have set regulations for

Volvo's XC60 car has a six-cylinder, 3.2-litre engine and is powered by a mix of 85% bio-ethanol and 15% petrol.

overall car fuel-efficiency at 38 miles per gallon, rising to 43mpg in 2008. In the EU, car manufacturers have committed to reducing the average emissions of their new cars to 140 grammes of CO_2 per km by 2008 and to 130g CO_2 per km by 2012. However, these targets aren't legally binding and the 2008 figure looks likely to be missed by a wide margin.

There is also an enormous amount of work to be done with regard to the energy efficiency of cars. Believe it or not, only about 15% of the energy from the fuel you put in your tank actually moves the car or powers accessories – the rest is lost to engine and design inefficiencies. The weight of the vehicle is a significant factor. However, new composite materials are helping to reduce weight and often improve safety as well. The energy efficiency guru Amory Lovins has even designed ultra-light-weight, aerodynamic "super cars", that could potentially achieve 300 miles per gallon.

But more efficient engine technology depends on cleaner gasoline and diesel: less advanced fuels would quickly gum up these sensitive engines. So one development can't happen without the other: new efficient engines need cleaner fuels and cleaner fuels are best used in modern engines. Hence the research and development work of fuel companies and automotive manufacturers.

Greener planes

Aviation is becoming a pariah industry in some sections of the media due to its large per passenger environmental impact. Plane manufacturers have made big improvements in fuel efficiency and emissions over the past thirty years, but there is plenty left to do. Each generation of planes will use lighter materials and more efficient and quieter engines. European manufacturers have set a target for new aircraft in 2020 to be 50% more efficient than aircraft built in 2000.

Cleaner fossil fuels

There are some fossil-fuel alternatives to petrol and diesel that can be better for the environment. Liquefied Petroleum Gas (LPG), a compressed blend of propane and butane, is extracted from either natural gas or crude oil. LPG produces 15% less CO_2 per kilometre than petrol does but is less energy-dense and will give you fewer kilometres per litre.

As for local pollution, LPG vehicles are generally comparable to modern petrol vehicles. As such, they can help in developing countries where low-sulphur fuels and modern engine technologies are not widely available, since it can be used in older engines. The main downside of LPG is that existing cars can't use it until they've undergone a relatively expensive conversion process.

Gas To Liquid (GTL) fuel, also made from natural gas (hence having the additional benefit of reducing dependence on oil), can be used in diesel vehicles, either neat or blended with regular diesel fuel. GTL is cleaner-burning and produces much less local pollution than both petrol and diesel, so has potential for helping congested cities combat air pollution. It is also a liquid at atmospheric pressure, so can be transported and used in today's infrastructure and vehicles. Advances in the manufacturing process could also make GTL a lower-carbon fuel than petrol or diesel.

Another possibility is Compressed Natural Gas (CNG), which can be used in petrol engines with few modifications. It helps with local air pollution but is not widely used because infrastructure requirements include needing a high-pressure gas cylinder in the vehicle.

Biofuels

Biofuels are fuels made from biomass. That usually means plants, though animal products and wastes can also be used. There are two main types of so-called first generation biofuels:

- Bioethanol is usually made from wheat, rapeseed, corn, soya and sugarcane, and used mainly in a mix with regular petrol.
- Biodiesel is usually made from rapeseed, palm oil and soybean oil, and used mainly in a blend with regular diesel.

Biofuels have been around for years – Henry Ford designed his Model T to run on them – but their uptake has been hampered by the fact that they've always been more expensive to produce than petrol or diesel. Today, however, many governments are actively encouraging biofuels, offering tax breaks, subsidies and setting mandatory targets. Governments are attracted in part by the prospect of being able to grow fuel locally and thereby reduce energy dependency – Brazil, for example, has been producing biofuel for nearly thirty years. And higher oil prices are making it more appealing.

Biofuels are also seen as a way to reduce the climate impact of transport. After all, the plants used to make the fuels absorb CO_2 when they grow. But biofuels are not carbon neutral. It

Researchers at Purdue University, USA have genetically modified cedar trees to be used as a renewable source of ethanol-based biofuel.

takes energy to grow and harvest the plants, and to process and distribute the resulting fuel. So the climate benefits depend on factors such as the crops selected and locations and practices of the farms that grow them. Bioethanol from sugarcane, for example, with its waste used for energy has a far smaller carbon footprint than the same fuel made from corn.

Perhaps the main question surrounding biofuels is how the demand for fuel crops could impact on markets for food crops and agricultural land. Biofuels have already been associated with rising food prices sufficient to cause riots in Mexico. And rising demand for palm oil and soya is also causing rain-forests to be cleared to make way for plantations in Malaysia, Brazil and Indonesia. This releases huge amounts of CO_2 and destroys habitats for endangered species such as the orang-utan.

"Second generation" biofuels could be a better solution. They can be made from non-food crops, like wood or straw, and can produce 90% less CO_2 than petrol and don't compete with food production for land. Unfortunately they are at least five years away from filling-station forecourts, as production trials on an industrial scale continue.

Hydrogen

Being clean and quiet at point of use, hydrogen is the holy grail of transport fuels. It is the most plentiful element in the universe and can be used to generate electricity in a fuel cell, producing only water and heat as by-products. Unfortunately, while hydrogen is everywhere, it's never found in its pure form, as it readily combines with other elements such as oxygen and carbon.

Though currently manufacturing costs are restrictively high, pure hydrogen can be created from natural gas or coal (a process that itself produces CO_2) or by passing an electric current through water, which again somewhat defeats the purpose, unless the electricity used comes from renewable sources. In the future it may be possible to capture the produced CO_2 and store it underground, although there are still various questions surrounding this technology (see p.38).

Also, because hydrogen is a completely new type of fuel, it would require an entirely new delivery infrastructure, which would need to be closely linked with the mass introduction of hydrogen fuelled vehicles. This would require the coordination of governments, energy producers, engine manufacturers and consumers. Moreover, though it can be used in modified combustion engines, to get the best results it should be used in fuel-cell vehicles. Prototypes already exist, but fuel-cell vehicles are still some way from mass production.

Government, vehicle makers and fuel producers are all keen to introduce hydrogen. Iceland hopes to become the first hydrogen economy, running all its cars, buses and fishing boats on the fuel. But the cost of the fuel cells and the making and distributing of hydrogen means that this transition is expected to take ten to twenty years. Interestingly, unlike petrol and diesel, which are produced in large refineries, there is an opportunity for hydrogen to be manufactured in smaller plants (or mini-networks) – particularly when sufficient electricity from renewable resources is available for splitting water into H_2 and O_2.

Heating and cooling

04

B uildings, such as homes and offices, use around a third of global energy. Of that third, a small proportion (18% in the EU and 24% in the US) is consumed by appliances and lights. The majority is used for heating and cooling rooms, and for heating water. The relative demands of heating and cooling depend on location. In northern Europe, for example, heating accounts for about two-thirds of all domestic energy consumption, whereas in hotter regions, such as the American Southwest, it's air conditioning, rather than heating, that's in demand.

In the developed world, most heating relies on gas or electricity (although in some areas, such as the north-eastern US, fuel oil is still important). In the developing world, however, millions of people still rely on wood and crop waste for heating (perhaps supplemented by kerosene). All of the latter create indoor pollution, which can have serious impacts on personal health, and some require time to be spent chopping and gathering.

Cooling in the developed world runs on electricity, but in

the warmer developing nations, it tends to rely on traditional passive design features. For example, many homes in hot desert climates have small windows and thick walls for insulation, and are painted white to reflect the sun and heat.

Heating and cooling homes

Modern homes in developed countries have central heating systems: typically either forced-air (heated by gas, oil or electricity and circulated through vents in the walls or floor); or by water heated in a boiler (fuelled by gas or electricity and pumped around the building, warming rooms when it passes through tubes in the floor or radiators on the walls). In rural areas not connected to the natural gas network, a forced-air furnace or boiler can be fuelled by propane, oil or wood, with hot water provided by an electric immersion system. In areas where electricity costs are low and gas networks limited – such as France, with its nuclear power, and Scandinavia and Switzerland, with their hydropower – electric radiators are widely used.

Not every home uses radiators or air ducts. In some homes concrete floors or walls radiate the heat from electric mats like those found in electric blankets or networks of hot water tubes buried in them.

While most homes have their own furnace or boiler, district heating is also a popular alternative in some cities, especially in Russia and various Nordic countries. Hot water or steam from a central plant (which is sometimes waste steam from electricity generation) is pumped around a neighbourhood and used to heat the buildings' central heating system. A variety of fuels can be used. However, this relies on the plant being in a heavily populated area, as heat loss increases dramatically with distance.

Hot countries have typically constructed buildings with integral design features to keep cool. But the use of electrically powered air conditioning in private homes is increasing, and it tends to be one of the first things families in warm climates aspire to as they become wealthier.

Heating and cooling offices

Large offices, shops and commercial buildings generally use large-scale central heating systems, again typically fuelled by a gas or oil-fired boiler. Keeping cool is a bigger problem for offices than homes, as they are often densely packed with people (giving off body heat) and computer equipment (emitting lots of waste heat); they are also occupied during the day, when the sun is hottest.

Many large modern offices have windows that, for safety reasons, cannot be opened, which means there is no natural ventilation. Therefore, most office buildings have central air-conditioning systems, powered by electricity or sometimes gas, that blow cool air around the building through a network of ducts. A few offices use other systems, such as river, groundwater or deep lake water cooling. For example, water from Lake Ontario is used to cool skyscrapers in Toronto's financial district.

More heat, more cooling

Economic growth means that more consumers are able to afford electrical appliances, and heating and cooling systems that were once considered luxuries. For example, urban ownership of air-conditioning units in China has dramatically increased: in 2005, there were 35 times as many households equipped with air conditioning as there were only a decade earlier. Room air conditioner purchases in India are currently growing at 20% per year, with about half of these purchases attributed to the residential sector. This brings improvements in personal comfort, but has wider energy implications. Since most heating and cooling consumes natural gas, oil or coal (either directly or indirectly), it contributes to climate change.

Hot improvements

Plenty can be done to make buildings more efficient in their use of heating and cooling and save us lots of money to boot. We often don't realise how much energy is being wasted or how much money is literally going out the window (or the uninsulated wall). An ICPP report of 2007 published an estimation that global CO_2 emissions from buildings' energy use could be reduced by about 30% by 2020 – at no net cost. It's even possible to construct homes and offices that don't need any conventional heating or cooling whatsoever – the German-designed Passivhaus is currently the best-known example (see p.76).

Existing buildings

Reducing the energy use of existing buildings is just as crucial as building new energy-efficient homes, but it is more expensive and more of a challenge. A lot can be done to improve energy efficiency through cost-effective improvements like installing double-glazing and insulation, but building regulations are essential to making this happen.

Since 2006 the European Union has required a "passport" to be provided by the owner when a building is sold or leased that specifies its energy efficiency – or lack of it. The hope is that this will encourage people to move to more energy-efficient homes, and put pressure on owners of poorer properties to improve them. However, the EU has had to issue infringement proceedings against almost every one of its member states: it's a measure of how unwilling the world's governments still are about enforcing such things.

New buildings

Most countries have regulations that set standards for the safety of buildings, and many also have energy efficiency standards but this requires enforcement on a national level to ensure builders build better homes in the first place. Without legal directives, few builders will take on the costs of building energy efficient homes because they will not benefit from the future savings – the owners (or renters) will.

The European Union has introduced an Energy Performance of Buildings Directive, which sets standards for both new and existing buildings, introduces certification schemes and requires regular inspections of boilers and air conditioning equipment. The US has extended its Energy Star scheme, which certifies America's most efficient appliances, to buildings. Many other countries, including giants such as China, are bringing in energy efficiency requirements.

Building design

Good design is the key to the energy efficiency of buildings. In cool climates, how much heating can be derived from sunlight and how much heat escapes from the building through draughts and poor insulation are the most significant factors. Ideally a building should have its longest axis running from east to west: a high length-to-width ratio helps because it maximizes exposure to the sun's warmth and light. In hot climates, windows work best on walls facing away from the sun: those facing the sun should be shaded by overhangs and trees to reduce solar heat. Basements or cellars below ground level are also useful because they create a "thermal reservoir" that prevents the building temperature swinging too much during the day. The colour of roofs and walls also helps – white absorbs less heat, which is why it is so common in hot regions.

Modern buildings can combine good ventilation with exceptional energy efficiency (via heat exchangers, for example), which make stale air, lack of ventilation and sick building syndrome things of the past. Designing buildings with natural ventilation reduces the need for air conditioning. That's doesn't simply mean having windows that open, but also having a chimney-like space such as an atrium that helps to move air around the building. Natural ventilation can also be used to bring in cooler air at night, which means there is less need for cooling during the day.

Good insulation in walls and roofs makes sure heat stays in – or out – depending on the need. Until fairly recently, many of the world's houses were built with cavity walls (an inner and outer wall with a gap between). Filling this cavity with insulating material can save 15% of heating energy in a temperate country such as the UK. Double- or triple-glazed, well-fitting windows make sure that little heat escapes, and that few draughts get in. Another 15% of a building's heating energy could be escaping through the roof in houses without proper loft insulation. Even if a building has loft insulation it may not be as effective as it could be: loft insulation to more stringent standards, properly enforced, could save a chunk of heating energy.

Building materials

These can also make a difference to the amount of heating or cooling that a building needs. The structure – floors and walls especially – stores heat, and dense material such as concrete is better than steel at doing that, which is one of the reasons why concrete floor heating is so efficient. Some commercial buildings use this property to reduce swings in indoor temperatures. Wood provides good insulation – and is carbon neutral when derived from sustainable sources. Every city in the world has its forest of glass-faced office towers, even though this is very inefficient in hot climates because it pushes up the energy used to cool the place. However, modern glass "superwindows" have been developed. Thanks to membranes that filter out only certain wavelengths of sunlight, they let light in but keep the heat out. Strategic use of shading and overhangs can also reduce absorption.

Lower-energy heaters and coolers

The energy efficiency of our heating systems will play a vital part in reducing the energy consumption of buildings, especially in energy-hungry offices. Most offices will also need some kind of cooling, but this can be less energy-intensive than traditional blower systems. For example, a chilled beam system can save around a fifth of cooling energy. It essentially works like a water-heating radiator – but using cold water and fitting radiators or pipes at ceiling rather than floor level, to cool the warm air that rises.

There are a range of increasingly energy-efficient heating and air-conditioning systems to choose from, and labelling schemes allow you to pick the best (see p.76). A modern natural gas boiler uses a third less energy than boilers fitted twenty years ago. These condensing boilers capture and use the waste heat in the flue gases, which makes them much more efficient. Further energy is saved if they are used to heat water at the moment it is required rather than keeping water hot in a tank all day until you wish to have a bath or shower. New technologies such as the home-sized combined heat and power unit (CHP) are becoming more affordable, and have the potential to dramatically cut home energy use. They are little power plants, burning gas to make electricity to send back to the grid and use the waste heat to warm your water and home (see p.46). You can also reduce your heating or cooling load by choosing models of fridges and lights that produce less heat than others, and controlling your

PassivHaus

PassivHaus is both a design standard and an organization that shows how to keep buildings at a comfortable temperature without using any conventional space heating or cooling. It reduces the total energy demands of a building to a 20th of the norm. The first to be built was in Germany in 1990 and there are now more than six thousand buildings around the world which meet the PassivHaus standard – offices as well as flats and houses, new and renovated buildings.

There are five key elements to the PassivHaus design:

1. The building "envelope" All components of the structure (floor, walls and roof) should be highly insulated

2. Airtightness Air leakage through unsealed joints is completely stopped

3. Ventilation A mechanical system is used to ventilate the building, also capturing warm heat as it is leaving so that it warms the cooler air coming in

4. Heat loss Losses from badly insulated points in windows, doors or other parts of the "envelope" are eliminated

5. Windows Heat loss is minimized in winter and heat gain minimized in summer

heating properly. The controls on our heating and cooling appliances are becoming increasingly sophisticated: boiler timing controls can be used to turn the heat only when you need it, and programmable air-conditioning thermostats can be used to stop rooms being cooler than they need to be. Each room in a house has its own temperature needs – a bedroom needn't be as warm as a living room, for instance. Thermostats can be fitted to each radiator or in each room to make sure you only heat or cool the rooms that need it. To state the obvious, energy that heats or cools a house when nobody is in it is energy wasted.

Some of the heat that builds up in the home and office is a wasteful side-effect of various appliances: incandescent lightbulbs, and electronic devices such as computers and printers are all culprits (see p.83). Choosing energy-efficient models and switching things off can make a significant difference to the amount of cooling that a building needs.

Human behaviour

The attitudes we take to heating and cooling our homes are another important part of the energy-saving equation. People who insist on being comfortable wandering around their homes with next to nothing on regardless of the time of year need much more heat than those who are prepared to dress according to the weather. In hot climates, air conditioning is often used in preference to simply opening a window – or overused to such an extent that people need to wear warmer clothes – a malaise particular rife in offices and shops. Furthermore, many people leave the air conditioning or heating on when they go on holiday.

Energy use is not just a response to climate conditions. Most people can be comfortable in a broader range of temperatures than homes and offices are often set to achieve. You won't be shivering in winter or wilting in summer if you change the thermostat by just 1°C – and that can save a tenth of the energy you use for heating or cooling.

05
Piecing it all together

Making the most of our resources

The world's demand for energy has increased dramatically over the last few decades, and will continue to do so (see p.10). Energy use is expected to double by 2050. Demand from developed nations will remain high while more energy, on a massive scale, will be required by developing nations to fuel their economic growth. Meeting this global demand will be a difficult enough task, even without the necessity of dealing with environmental issues such as climate change.

CO_2 emissions have tripled to seven gigatonnes (billion tonnes) per year since 1950. If they continue to grow at the same rate they are expected to double again – to fourteen gigatonnes per year – by 2050. To reduce the likelihood of a dangerous level of climate change – a temperature increase of 2.4 degrees or more – we need to cut our global emissions substantially below that 7Gt as soon as possible. There is no single way to achieve these cuts, but a combination of many will contribute. Technological advances and energy conservation will play a vital role but in order for the scientists' work to bear fruit, governments, business and consumers all need to play a part.

Wedge theory

Breaking down the problem of climate change into identifiable and achievable parts was the approach suggested by Princeton University's Stephen Pacala and Robert H. Socolow: the wedge model. They demonstrated that there are various different ways of achieving a CO_2 reduction target and they represented the contributions as wedges. Each wedge represents action such as improving energy efficiency, developing alternative energy sources, low-emission transport options, or CO_2 capture and storage. Each emission-reduction strategy, or wedge, contributes a chunk of CO_2 to the reduction target (1Gt for each wedge). Different wedge combinations can come up with the desired reduction in emissions by the target date. It stimulates thinking about costs, the pace of change, risks and trade-offs.

In a nutshell, the main energy-related wedges are: improvements to energy efficiency; lower carbon sources of electricity; and lower carbon fuels for transport.

Energy efficiency

Becoming more energy efficient – as opposed to merely producing more energy – is clearly the most cost-effective single step. An increase in energy efficiency means we can get more – more development, more energy services – without needing more energy.

Introducing mandatory energy efficiency standards in the construction of buildings, or in the performance of electrical appliances can also make a big difference. The best modern homes and offices use far less energy than standard new buildings; some are even net energy producers, sending electricity back to the grid. But simply installing compact fluorescent bulbs in all of the world's fifty billion light fixtures would provide a third of a wedge in itself.

As explained on p.57, there is also huge room for improvement in car manufacturing: vehicle fuel efficiency hasn't improved much since the 1980s – which is not surprisingly the last time governments introduced fuel efficiency standards on carmakers' fleets. One proposed 1Gt wedge could be cut if two billion of the world's cars could run at an efficiency of sixty miles per gallon (as opposed to 30mpg).

Raising the conversion efficiency of existing coal-fired power plants so that they turn 60% of the fuels energy into electricity (instead of 40% today), while halving the energy used during fossil fuel extraction, processing and delivery to those plants, would also constitute a wedge.

Energy	Washing machine
Manufacturer Model	

More efficient
A
B
C
D
E
F
G
Less efficient

Energy consumption kWh/cycle	1.55
Based on standard load washing at 60°C normal cycle	
Actual energy consumption will depend on how the appliance is used	

Washing performance A higher G lower	A BCDEFG
Spin drying performance A higher G lower Spin speed (rpm)	A B CDEFG 1400
Capacity (cotton) kg Water consumption	5.0 5.5
Noise (dB(A) re 1 pW) Washing Spinning	5.2 7.6

Further information is contained in product brochure

New EU label
Lovingly recreated by 2.1 Mark and Simon

Lower carbon electricity

Cleaner fossil fuels

New, cleaner technologies are being developed and their costs reduced all the time. But even once they achieve cost competitiveness, they will take time to bring in on a large scale. Which means that, given the world's current energy mix, infrastructure and distribution networks, it makes sense to make the most of our natural gas resources. Natural gas is a cleaner option among fossil fuels, producing around half as much CO_2 as coal and far fewer local air pollutants. It is also much more energy efficient: gas power stations turn more energy into electricity than coal-fired generators. Quadrupling the use of natural gas in power plants, replacing an equal number of coal-fired plants, would provide a 1Gt wedge.

Another wedge might be provided by carbon capture and storage, or CCS, technology (see p.38). Carbon dioxide can be removed either before or after the fuel is burnt and then buried deep below the earth's surface, or beneath the sea-bed. CCS also has clear implications for the coal industry, when you consider the concentrated CO_2 emissions of coal-fired power plants. It will require a massive amount of investment – in building new plants or adapting existing ones – for it to make a difference.

Renewables and nuclear power

In the long term, more and more of our energy could be derived from **renewable energy sources**. Replacing power derived from coal plants with 300,000 5MW wind turbines would account for one wedge. This number of turbines would require an area around the size of Portugal. But the land beneath them could, of course, be used for grazing or farming. And, furthermore, advances in cable technology, such as High Voltage Direct

Current (HVDC) transmission lines, allow electricity to cross thousands of kilometres with minimal losses, which would allow the installation of wind turbines a long way offshore. Photovoltaic solar energy, derived from solar panels, could also provide a wedge. It would require a 700-fold expansion of solar energy, replacing coal. As with wind energy, the sheer physical space these would take up is a challenge, but it is not an impossible one. Solar panels are typically mounted on walls and roofs, and, again, HVDC technology will allow electricity to be carried across long distances from the planet's sunniest areas – which are often also the least populated ones. As ever, investment is necessary for such technologies to work. And, furthermore, no small amount of political will.

Although nuclear power is controversial, largely due to the problems of storing radioactive waste, it could provide a further wedge, were we to triple the amount of energy currently generated by nuclear sources by adding about seven hundred one-gigawatt plants as well as maintaining or improving all nuclear plants now in use.

Lower carbon fuels

Carbon capture and storage, described above, is a technology with plenty of implications for the transport industry. While hydrogen could fuel vehicles without releasing any CO_2 (see p.63), CO_2 is still released in the process of extracting the hydrogen from coal or natural gas in the first place. Using CCS, however, this CO_2 could be captured: hydrogen vehicles would then be running on a fuel with virtually no carbon footprint. Alternatively, an integrated low-carbon energy strategy could use renewable or nuclear power sources to generate the electricity needed to manufacture hydrogen.

Furthermore, Socolow believes that CCS could also provide another wedge, in cleaning up production at synfuel plants, which generate a synthetic fuel from coal. Obtaining fuels from coal is significantly more carbon-intensive than obtaining fuels from crude oil and could well become more numerous as oil becomes harder to extract.

Biofuels present another way we can find a wedge: if we were to scale up current global ethanol production by fifty times, for instance. This would indisputably be quite a challenge: using current practices, one wedge would require planting an area the size of India with biofuel crops by 2055 – equivalent to one-sixth of the world's crop land.

Making it happen

Governments

It's clear that there are many ways to increase energy efficiency and cut emissions. But knowing how to do this and actually making it happen are two very different things. As long as these technologies cost more than the current status quo, it's unlikely that businesses or consumers will adopt them voluntarily. There's one vital ingredient lacking – political will. With unprecedented challenges posed by energy security and climate change, the need to seize opportunities to address global demands is more pressing than ever.

For one thing, the governments of the world need to coordinate their efforts. International governmental cooperation will be necessary to introduce renewable energy sources – creating the distribution networks and sharing the technology to make them sufficiently inexpensive to be viable. For example, a German study has posited that 80% of Europe's electricity could be produced from renewable power by using high voltage direct current cables to link the networks of all the countries in Europe and connect them to large-scale sources of wind and solar power in North Africa and geothermal-based hydrogen in Iceland.

The Kyoto Protocol, a United Nations treaty introduced in 1997, is probably the most talked-about example of inter-governmental coordination on energy issues – from an environmental perspective, at least. It aimed to stabilize greenhouse gases, and set a target for participating developed nations of a collective average reduction of 5% below 1990 levels.

Kyoto has, however, fallen short of its modest goals. This is partly because some of the world's biggest polluters, such as the US and Australia, did not ratify it at the time, and partly because many of the countries who did will miss their 2012 targets. Furthermore China – now the world's biggest single polluter – received no binding limitations (on the grounds that it was not among the main contributors during the industrialisation process responsible for climate change). A post-2012 programme was negotiated in 2007 at the Bali conference. After much wrangling, a roadmap was eventually drawn up for a new agreement on "deep" emissions cuts, with a 2009 deadline. It was also decided that a fund should be set up to help poor countries adapt to the effects of climate change, such as droughts and flooding. However, no binding targets on reductions were set, and no decision was made on how the burden of combating climate change would be shared between developed and developing countries.

But beyond international goals and agreements, the domestic policies of governments need to support and provide incentives for the measures outlined earlier: increasing energy efficiency, switching to natural gas, cleaning up fossil fuels and using renewable sources. Governments can also help by encouraging a shift to lower CO_2 energy by market mechanisms. Carbon taxes, for example, can send a price signal by making energy that releases more CO_2 more expensive. Innovation can also be supported by targeted subsidies for investment, which would help propel

UNFCCC Executive Secretary Yvo de Boer (left) and UN Secretary General Ban Ki-moon (right) at the UN Framework Convention on Climate Change, Bali.

markets towards solutions that are friendlier to the environment. Likewise, schemes such as carbon trading (see box overleaf), allocations, penalties and incentives can alter consumer and producer behaviour via market mechanisms. These could help to create the conditions that will support transformations in the energy sector. At the same time government policies can make stricter demands on the efficiency of appliances and vehicles, and impose tighter regulations on new buildings, for example.

Industry

Governments can create conditions for industry to innovate. It is the energy industry, working with vehicle manufacturers and equipment suppliers, that has the experience, expertise and resources to develop new technologies. The business world does acknowledge the scale of the task ahead. The World Business

Emissions trading: CO_2 in the EU

The theory of emissions trading is that the "right to pollute" is turned into a saleable commodity, providing a market incentive for companies and nations to reduce their greenhouse gas emissions. The idea has a precedent in the US's sulphur trading scheme of the 1990s, which not only achieved its target cut but so much more cheaply than predicted.

The European Union launched the first large-scale attempt to trade CO_2 allowances in 2005. Here's how it works. The EU agrees maximum annual emissions – the cap – for each participating country, which then allocates that, in the form of permits, to industrial companies. Companies with emissions below their caps can sell the surplus permits. Companies who cannot meet their caps have to buy surpluses from other companies to make up the difference. This trading in carbon emissions permits means that companies (and countries) will invest in reducing their CO_2 emissions if the cost of doing so is less than buying other companies' surpluses in the market.

Companies invest in the most cost-effective projects first and, since scarcity makes a commodity more expensive, there ought to be a strong incentive for a company to invest in carbon credits.

So far, the environmental efficacy of the EU's carbon trading scheme has been hampered by caps that have been set far too low, which has made it too easy for companies to hit their targets. However, steps have now been taken to tighten allocations for the next period of trading. National allocations will be an average of 7% lower, all GHGs will count (not just CO_2) and aviation emissions are currently also expected to be factored in. As a result prices have risen.

Council for Sustainable Development (WBCSD), a CEO-led association of some two hundred companies, has examined the feasibility of various reduction scenarios and it come up with several 1Gt CO_2 "wedges" that are comparable to the measures outlined earlier, emphasizing the necessity of more efficient use of energy in buildings, more efficient appliances, implementation of CCS (see p.38), replacing oil and coal with natural gas and renewable energy sources, increased use of public transport, and the manufacture of hydrogen-fuelled cars.

Industry, however, is ultimately guided by the rules set by governments and by the demands of consumers. Political parties – in democracies at least – are also ultimately steered by the promptings of voters and the media. Which is where the ordinary citizen and consumer come into the picture.

What you can do as an energy consumer

There is plenty that consumers in developed nations can do every day to save energy and reduce CO_2 emissions. Our own personal actions might not seem like much, but collectively it all makes a big difference. And it doesn't mean freezing in the dark. There are two broad strands: use less energy, and make sure what you use involves as little carbon as possible whether at home or in the office.

In your home life

Energy efficiency, like charity, begins at home. Most people could use less electricity with little impact on their lifestyle. Here's how:

- Use energy efficient light bulbs. They use no more than a quarter of the energy of old-style "incandescent" bulbs, and are available in a wide range of styles.
- Hit the A-list when buying new appliances. The A to E ratings in many countries make it easy to choose energy efficiency.
- Switch off – TV, stereo, DVD players and computer equipment waste energy on standby. Switch them off at the wall. Turn off lights when leaving a room.

- Turn down the thermostat and wear a sweater if it's cold outside. Similarly, in hot climates, there's no point in air conditioning making buildings so cold that you need to wear a sweater.
- Insulate the roof properly and insulate your hot water tank, or even better, replace it with a condensing combination boiler that heats water on demand. If building a new house or renovating an old, look into installing solar water heaters or solar power panels, or earth heating and cooling.
- Draught-proof windows and doors, replacing old windows with double-glazing.
- Do you really need air conditioning? Shade windows from the hot sun, fit ceiling fans to push warm air towards the ceiling in summer and downwards into the room in winter.

Travel is, of course, a serious source of GHG emissions, and few people travel in the most energy efficient way.

- Walk or cycle to the shop, bar or station instead of driving. You know you need the exercise so cycle to work or take public transport.
- Switch to a smaller, lighter, more fuel-efficient car, or join a car-sharing scheme.
- Take fewer flights. Cut back on long-haul travel and for short breaks favour locations accessible by train. When you do fly, look for airlines flying the latest, most fuel-efficient planes.

At the office

There's a great deal you can do in terms of behaviour and encouraging your employer to be energy conscious:

- Encourage your workplace to cut down on needless long-haul business trips and make use of videoconferencing using webcams or facilities like Apple Mac's iChat or Skype.

- Suggest your business participates in recycling schemes, and includes energy efficient measures when moving or considering office alterations.
- When you leave for the day switch your computer off and turn off the lights if you are the last one in the office. Better yet, make sure your facilities manager gets the cleaners to do so when they leave at night.

Make yourself heard

Governments across the world need to respond to concerns over environment and over energy. If you think they are making the wrong decisions (or even the right ones), then let them know. It has never been easier to get your views across and the Resources section of this book will show you plenty of helpful websites to look at. You can write or email politicians, whether national or local. You can start a blog or a website and direct people to it so as to put pressure on those in charge. If they don't know you care it will be easier for them not to act, and just to hope that things will sort themselves out in the distant future. They won't.

Your power as a consumer can be used to support those companies whether traditional or alternative that have the best environmental policies or are the most committed to finding creative energy solutions. Utilize your spending power wisely to support the products or the shares of companies that convince you they may be helping the planet, or at worst not damaging it. The responsibility for our energy needs and our planet is ultimately everybody's. The way forward won't be easy. But everybody can help.

Resources

Further Reading

Energy

Energy at the Crossroads: Global Perspectives and Uncertainties, Vaclav Smil (MIT Press, 2005). Smil provides a thorough history of energy production in the twentieth century, before examining the effect energy issues have on the economy, on quality of life, and on the environment.

Energy and Security: Toward a New Foreign Policy Strategy, ed. Jan H. Kalicki (Johns Hopkins University Press, 2005). A collection of essays by different experts examining the relationship of the US with the producer nations that it depends upon.

The Final Energy Crisis, ed. by Andrew McKillip with Sheila Newman (Pluto Press, 2005) International collection of essays examining various aspects of over-reliance on fossil fuels.

Future Energy: How the New Oil Industry Will Change People, Politics, and Portfolios, Bill Paul (Wiley, 2007). If energy demand, as many suggest, is one of the best business opportunities of all time, what will people be investing in?

Half Gone: Oil, Gas, Hot Air, and the Global Energy Crisis, Jeremy Leggett (Portobello Books, 2005). Dwindling oil supplies and global warming collide in this expert explanation by geological consultant turned Greenpeace activist.

The New Energy Paradigm, ed. Dieter Helm (Oxford University Press, 2007). An overview of the current energy policy debate, addressing environmental issues and considering how international energy markets effect security of supply.

Sustainable Fossil Fuels: the Unusual Suspect in the Quest for Clean and Enduring Energy, Mark Jaccard (Cambridge University Press, 2005). The case for the potential of fossil fuels to be turned into clean, sustainable energy sources.

Climate Change

The Economics of Climate Change, Sir Nicholas Stern (Cambridge University Press, 2007). The much-discussed UK report that soberly addressed how much climate change could cost.

The Rough Guide to Climate Change, Robert Henson (Rough Guides, 2006). Everything you need to know about climate change.

The Rough Guide to Ethical Living, Duncan Clark (Rough Guides, 2006). Low-carbon living and responsible shopping.

On DVD

A Crude Awakening Frank Messmer's documentary examining peak oil theory and the impact it would have on our oil-dependent society.

The 11th Hour, narrated by Leonardo DiCaprio, picks up where *An Inconvenient Truth* left off by presenting solutions to climate change.

The End of Suburbia: Oil Depletion and the Collapse of the American Dream explains how the American lifestyle has become dependent on cars and oil.

An Inconvenient Truth Al Gore's landmark documentary explaining what climate change is and how we can stop it.

Who Killed the Electric Car? Chris Paine and Martin Sheen's documentary looks at how the electric car was developed and subsequently dropped in the late 1990s, exploring the complex political, economic and scientific reasons for this.

Websites

General information

How Stuff Works www.howstuffworks.com

As you might expect, this provides detailed explanations of how things work, from the electric grid and photovoltaic cells to fuel cells and wind turbines.

Governments and academics

Energy Information Administration www.eia.doe.gov

Official energy statistics from the US dept of energy.

Intergovernmental Panel on Climate Change www.ipcc.ch

The IPCC is a UN body whose role is to assess the scientific basis of human-induced climate change by assessing scientific, technical, and socio-economic research.

International Energy Agency www.iea.org

The IEA represents 26 industrialised countries that have agreed to share energy information and cooperate on "rational energy programmes" – such as reducing dependence on oil and ensuring an effective response to future oil emergencies. It publishes the comprehensive annual forecasting paper, World Energy Outlook.

The Tyndall Centre for Climate Change Research www.tyndall.ac.uk

Academic centre promoting a sustainable response to climate change in the UK and internationally.

United Nations Development Programme www.undp.org/energy

Home of the United Nations' energy-related sustainable development projects.

US Department of Energy www.energy.gov

A prime source for statistics and reports on energy research commissioned by the US government.

The Energy Industry

BP Statistical Review www.bp.com

Compiles data voluntarily submitted from right across the energy industries.

European Nuclear Society www.euronuclear.org

International federation of 26 societies that promote and advance science and engineering for the peaceful use of nuclear energy.

Hubbert Peak of Oil Production www.hubbertpeak.com

Data, analysis, and recommendations regarding the "impending peak of global oil extraction".

Shell www.shell.com

Information on the company's contribution to meeting future energy needs.

World Business Council for Sustainable Development (WBCSD) www.wbcsd.org

A CEO-led, global association of around 200 companies dealing with business and sustainable development. The Council provides a platform for companies to explore sustainable development. Publishes an annual review and other statistics.

Campaigners, pressure groups and NGOs

Climate Action Network www.climatenetwork.org A worldwide network of over 365 Non-Governmental Organisations that promote action to keep human-induced climate change within ecologically sustainable levels.

Friends of the Earth www.foei.org

Greenpeace www.greenpeace.org

George Monbiot www.monbiot.com An excellent resource for keeping up with current developments on climate change, energy usage, and social justice.